Controversies in Post Keynesian Economics

To Christopher, Arik, and Emily who probably would have preferred a book with pictures.

Controversies in Post Keynesian Economics

Paul Davidson

Holly Chair of Excellence in Political Economy
University of Tennessee

Edward Elgar

Published by
Edward Elgar Publishing Limited
Gower House
Croft Road
Aldershot
Hants GU11 3HR
England

Edward Elgar Publishing Company
Old Post Road,
Brookfield
Vermont 05036
USA

British Library Cataloguing in Publication Data
Davidson, Paul *1930–*
   Controversies in Post Keynesian economics.
   1. Economics. Post Keynesian theories.
   I. Title
   330.15

Library of Congress Cataloguing in Publication Data
Davidson, Paul.
      Controversies in post keynesian economics / Paul Davidson.
         p.   cm.
      1. Keynesian economics. 2. Neoclassical school of economics.
   3. Chicago school of economics.   I. Title.
   HB99.7.D39   1991
   330.15'7–dc20   90-46793
                                                                  CIP
   ISBN 1 85278 366 4
         1 85278 375 3 (paperback)

Printed in Great Britain by Billing & Sons Ltd, Worcester

Contents

Introduction

What exactly was the 'Keynesian Revolution'? Was it really a revolution in the way economists and policy-makers think about real-world economic problems? Since John Maynard Keynes wrote his *General Theory* over a half-century ago, can his analysis still be relevant to the world of the twenty-first century into which we are about to enter?

These questions have often been debated amongst economists. Most professional economic discussions rarely have reached a conclusion – and the academic discussions involving these particular queries are no exception. For students and intelligent laypeople, it must seem almost inconceivable that economists – who often try to portray themselves as 'scientists' – can be in such disarray. With this book, I hope to provide some perspective to the reader as to why economists seem unable to agree on almost anything, and especially about the meaning and importance of the Keynesian revolution.

Our approach will be to review and analyse, from a 1990s' perspective, the debates among differing schools of economic thought – the monetarists, the [neoclassical] Keynesians, and the Post Keynesians – regarding the pressing problems of our times: unemployment and inflation. We will explain, in simple language, the philosophical and axiomatic differences (and similarities) in the logical foundations of these schools and the sociological interactions that developed between generations of economists.

The resulting history of the development of the economics discipline since the Second World War involved a struggle for the minds of economists, policy-makers, central bankers, and ultimately the mass media. Our story involves how this struggle evolved, and why it aborted the Keynesian revolution in economic analysis, despite the latter's relevance for the money-using entrepreneurial economies in which we live. We shall show why reality and obvious universal truths were rejected by neoclassical economists intent on developing a precise, but fictional, analysis.

A study of the debates and the events of the 1970s will indicate why the neoclassical Keynesians lost their credibility in the profession of economics and their influence on presidents and central bankers. The eagerly waiting monetarists moved into the power vacuum only to be thrown over by the events of the 1980s. In the 1990s, economic theory is, despite disclaimers by the economics establishment, in ruins. Economists, who were revered almost as medical doctors (to the economic body) for their successes of the 1940s and 1950s as they followed the policy prescriptions of Keynes – even when they did not understand his theoretical analysis – are looked upon with increasing disdain in the 1990s as their advice seems more and more irrelevant. Yet, in truth, we will only get our economic policy right when we get our economic theory right. We cannot always hope to be lucky or muddle through when economic problems rear their ugly heads. Too much of the welfare of mankind is involved.

Hopefully the reader will obtain, from this book, a sense of what a proper economic analysis of the world that we inhabit must rest on. Economics, unlike some sciences, involves things that each of us pursue in almost all of our waking hours. And, for better or for worse, our actions can create our individual economic destinies as well as that of our society. If we fail to understand the economics principles which govern our lives, we can threaten our own economic survival by advocating foolish economic policies and actions.

1. The Need for a Theoretical Revolution

On New Year's Day in 1935 the English economist, John Maynard Keynes, wrote a letter to George Bernard Shaw, in which he stated:

> To understand my new state of mind, however, you have to know that I believe myself to be writing a book on economic theory which will largely revolutionize not I suppose at once but in the course of the next ten years the way the world thinks about economic problems. When my new theory has been duly assimilated and mixed with politics and feelings and passions, I cannot predict what the final upshot will be in its effect on actions and affairs, but there will be a great change and in particular the Ricardian Foundations of Marxism will be knocked away. I can't expect you or anyone else to believe this at the present stage, but for myself I don't merely hope what I say. In my own mind I am quite sure.[1]

A little over a year later, Keynes published a book which was to revolutionize the way economists and, ultimately, politicians develop economic policies to deal with unemployment. That book was entitled *The General Theory of Employment, Interest, and Money*.

Keynes had started working on this book in 1932. Great Britain, unlike the United States, had been suffering from a deep recession almost since the end of the First World War. By 1932 there had been at least a decade of high unemployment. In fact, between 1922 and 1936, the rate of unemployment in Britain fell to below 10 per cent in only one year – in 1927, when it was 9.7 per cent. No wonder that English economists were more worried about the problem of chronic and persistent unemployment at the beginning of the 1930s than were their American counterparts.

In the United States the 'roaring twenties' had been a period of unbridled prosperity, which seemed to have become the American way of life. In 1929, only 3.2 per cent of American workers were unemployed, the stock market had continued to climb to unprecedented highs, and everybody was becoming rich. Just a few days before the stock market crash of 24 October 1929, one of the most eminent economists of that time, Professor Irving Fisher of Yale University, told an audience that the stock market had reached a high plateau from which it could only go up! Then, suddenly, the bottom fell out. It is said that Professor Fisher who, so to speak, put his money where his mouth was, lost between $8 million and $10 million in the stock market crash. The Great Depression had hit America!

From 1929 through 1933 the American economy went downhill. It seemed as if the system was enmeshed in a catastrophe from which it could not escape. By 1933, unemployment had climbed to 24.9 per cent, with one out of every four workers unemployed. A measure of the US standard of living, the real gross national product per capita, fell by 52 per cent between 1929 and 1933, so that, by 1933, the average American family was living on less than half of what it had consumed in 1929. The American capitalist dream appeared to be shattered.

The economic experts of those times, including Professor Irving Fisher, argued that the high levels of unemployment experienced in the United States in the early 1930s could not persist. The basis for this view of professional economists and politicians that unemployment could never be anything but a temporary aberration in a free market economy was something called neoclassical economic theory. This neoclassical analysis provided the rationale for the *laissez-faire* or 'no government intervention' philosophy which dominated economic discussions before Keynes's *General Theory* was published. The theory held that if everyone was motivated by self-interest, then what the Scottish economist, Adam Smith, had called, in 1776, the 'invisible hand' of the marketplace would assure that the economic system would experience full employment and stable prices. It was against this neoclassical 'invisible hand' theory that Keynes believed his book would revolutionize how economists perceived the actual operations of a market economy.

The United Kingdom had been in a continual slump since the end of the First World War. Since the early 1920s, Keynes had been warning his professional colleagues that neoclassical theory which assured a long-run full employment outcome for a *laissez-faire* economic system was both misleading and dangerous. In one of his most famous quotes regarding the neoclassicists' claim that free markets assure a long-run full employment, stable price situation, Keynes said:

> ...this long-run is a misleading guide to current affairs. In the long run we are all dead. Economists set themselves too easy, too useless a task if in tempestuous seasons they can only tell us that when the storm is long past, the ocean is flat again.[2]

Keynes specifically questioned the relevance of a *laissez-faire* philosophy for modern democratic capitalist systems in his 1926 article entitled 'The End of Laissez Faire'. In this essay he wrote:

> Let us clear from the ground the metaphysical or general principles upon which, from time to time, *laissez-faire* has been founded. It is *not* true that individuals possess a prescriptive 'natural liberty' in their economic activities. There is *no* 'compact' conferring perpetual rights on those who Have or on those who Acquire. The world is *not* governed from above so that private and social interest always coincide. It is *not* managed here below that in practice they coincide. It is *not* a correct deduction from the principles of economics that enlightened self-interest generally *is* enlightened; more often individuals acting separately to promote their own ends are too ignorant or too weak to attain even these. Experience does *not* show that individuals when they make up a social unit, are always less clear-sighted than when they act separately.[3]

In 1930, in the midst of the worldwide economic slump, Keynes again suggested that a *laissez-faire* approach not only may have contributed to the depression but might also be aggravating the situation when he wrote:

...what has occurred is not exactly an accident; it is deeply rooted in our general way of doing things.... If we leave matters to cure themselves, the results may be disastrous....This is a dangerous enterprise in a society which is both capitalist and democratic.[4]

Neoclassical economic theory attempted to demonstrate that a market economy, operating without any government regulation or interference, results in the best of all possible economic worlds. The Marquis d'Argenson, in 1751, claimed as the first writer to use the phrase *laissez-faire* in his argument for removing government from economic affairs, said that 'To govern better one must govern less'. Although the phrase *laissez-faire* does not appear in the writings of the founding fathers of neoclassical theory such as Adam Smith or David Ricardo, the idea is there. The pursuit of self-interest, unfettered by government interference is at the heart of the philosophy of neoclassical economics. In his 1776 classic, *The Wealth of Nations*, Adam Smith wrote:

It is not from the benevolence of the butcher, the brewer, or the baker that we expect our dinner, but from regard to their own self-interest. We address ourselves, not to their humanity but to their self love, and never talk to them of our necessities, but of their advantage...Every individual is continually exerting himself to find out the most advantageous employment for whatever capital he can command. It is his own advantage, indeed and not that of society which he has in view... He intends only his own gain, and he is in this, as in many other cases, led by an invisible hand to promote an end which was no part of his intention. By pursuing his own interest he frequently promotes that of the society more effectually than when he really intends to promote it.[5]

Accordingly, this philosophy holds that, during a period of unemployment, government economic intervention will only lead to a deterioration. If, on the other hand, the government did not interfere with the invisible hand of the market processes that were occurring during The Great Depression, only the weak and the inefficient would be weeded out, leaving a stronger and more powerful economy. In true Social Darwinian fashion, neoclassical theory asserted that what was occurring was a case of 'survival of the fittest' and, once the economic system had righted itself and regenerated full employment and prosperity for all, it would be even stronger than before.

In the very first paragraph of his book, *The General Theory*, Keynes wrote:

> I have called this book the *General Theory of Employment Interest and Money*.... The object of such a title is to contrast the character of my arguments and conclusions with those of the [neo]classical theory of the subject ... which dominates economic thought, both practical and theoretical of the governing and academic classes of this generation, as it has for a hundred years past.... The characteristics of the special case assumed by the [neo]classical theory happen not to be those of the economic society in which we actually live, with the result that its teaching is misleading and disastrous if we attempt to apply it to the facts of experience.[6]

In current times, Nobel Prize-winning economist James Tobin of Yale has said of Keynes's approach:

> John Maynard Keynes had the audacity to claim the discovery of massive, endemic, possible chronic market failure.... Keynes was quite explicit in this contention, opposing his 'general theory' to what he called 'classical' theory....He clearly meant theory that would now be called 'neoclassical'.[7]

NOTES

1. *The Collected Writings of John Maynard Keynes*, vol. XIII, Macmillan, London, 1971, p. 492.
2. J. M. Keynes, *A Tract on Monetary Reform* (1923); reprinted as vol. IV, *The Collected Writings of John Maynard Keynes*, op. cit. Quotation is on p. 65 of reprint.
3. *The Collected Writings of John Maynard Keynes*, vol. XI, op. cit., pp. 287–8.
4. J. M. Keynes, *A Treatise on Money* (1930), reprinted as vol. VI, *The Collected Writings of John Maynard Keynes*, op. cit., pp. 345–6.
5. Adam Smith, *An Inquiry into The Wealth of Nations*, Modern Library Edition, New York, 1937, p. 14.
6. J. M. Keynes, *The General Theory of Employment, Interest and Money*, Harcourt Brace, New York, 1936, p. 3.

7.   J. Tobin, 'Theoretical Issues In Macroeconomics', in G. R. Feiwel (ed.), *Issues in Contemporary Macroeconomics and Distribution*, State University of New York Press, Albany, 1985, p. 110.

2. Policy Prescriptions: Neoclassical Theory vs Keynes's Economic Reality

The neoclassical belief that a free enterprise system inevitably generates full employment and prosperity was grounded in an old economic proposition known as Say's Law. In 1803, a French economist, Jean Baptiste Say, wrote that 'products always exchange for products'. In 1808, the English economist, James Mill, translated Say's dictum as 'supply creates its own demand' – and this phraseology has since been established in economics as Say's Law. It was this economic law which Keynes railed against in his *General Theory*.

In plain terms we can explain what 'supply creates its own demand' means as follows. People produce – that is, supply – things to the market in order to earn income to buy (demand) other things from the market. Accordingly, Mill's interpretation of Say's Law implied that there could never be a depression, for the very act of production created sufficient income to purchase everything that was produced. Equally, there could never be unemployment since businessmen seeking profits would always be able to find sufficient demand to sell any output produced by workers. In a Say's Law world, ultimately, goods exchanged for goods. Money, in Mill's words, 'is only a veil' behind which the real economy operates unhampered by financial considerations. Changes in the money supply could therefore not affect the real dimensions of the economy such as the employment level and the production of goods.

Modern economists call the total production of all the nation's industries the Gross National Product (GNP). Since the real economy operates independent of the money supply in this 'money

7

is a veil' view, then it logically follows that any increase in the quantity of money would merely push up prices. Every additional increase in the money supply must cause inflation which, as well-worn economic homily states, is always the result of 'too much money chasing too few goods'.

Over time, Mill's view of 'money as a veil' has been accepted as a fundamental tenet of neoclassical economics and, by the early twentieth century, it had become *the* prevailing orthodoxy in economics textbooks. As economic theory developed a more 'scientific' foundation, the concept of 'money as a veil' was translated into a technical axiom called the neutrality of money, which presumes that money does not affect employment and the production of goods and services.

The dictionary defines an axiom as 'a statement universally accepted as true.... a statement that needs no proof because its truth is obvious'. Accordingly, for those who approach the study of economics through neoclassical theory, the belief in the neutrality of money is a fundamental axiom, an article of faith, requiring no proof or justification. Just as a religious person needs no proof of the existence of a Divine Being and will reject any evidence, 'scientific' or otherwise, which purports to demonstrate that there is no God, so do neoclassical economists deny that money can be shown to be ultimately non-neutral. Any evidence which purports to demonstrate that changes in the quantity of money *per se* can affect the real economy must be rejected by neoclassical theorists if they are to remain logically within their analytical framework.

Yet Keynes, and the current school of Post Keynesian economists who claim to follow Keynes's analytical lead, have developed a system which rejects the neutrality of money – and hence Say's Law – as a principle applicable to a market system where money is used as a means of settling contractual obligations.

For example, in 1933, Keynes drew the following distinction between neoclassical theory and the 'General Theory' upon which he was working:

An economy which uses money but uses it merely as a *neutral* link between transactions in real things and real assets and does not allow it to enter into motives or decisions, might be called – for want of a better name – a *real-exchange economy*. The theory which I desiderate would deal, in contradistinction to this, with an economy in which money plays a part of its own and affects motives and decisions and is, in short, one of the operative factors in the situation, so that the course of events cannot be predicted either in the long period or in the short, without a knowledge of the behavior of money between the first state and the last. And it is this which we ought to mean when we speak of *a monetary economy*...

Booms and depressions are peculiar to an economy in which ... *money is not neutral*. I believe that the next task is to work out in some detail such a monetary theory of production. That is the task on which I am now occupying myself in some confidence that I am not wasting my time.[1]

Keynes, therefore, was developing a general theory which rejected a fundamental neoclassical axiom – the neutrality of money – which had been the basis for economic theory for the previous 125 years, ever since Mill's introduction of Say's Law into English economics. No wonder that Keynes's 'General Theory' was considered revolutionary, if not heretical, for it struck at the very foundation of neoclassical faith –– the universal truth of the neutrality of money. No wonder, also, that Keynes's analysis and the further elaboration and evolution of Keynes's system by Post Keynesians has not been readily accepted by the majority of economists trained in the neoclassical tradition. The Keynes–Post Keynesian logic denied the most cherished neoclassical assertion of the neutrality of money and hence the conclusion that a free enterprise economy, in the long run, always assures full employment for all those who want to work. It is as antithetical to the neoclassical philosophy as the views on the origin of human life as asserted by the 'scientific theory of evolution' are to the 'scientific creationism' Biblical view of some fundamentalist Protestant religions.

However, the worldwide slump of the 1930s, meant that politicians and practical men throughout the world were willing to take desperate measures to save their civilizations. During the four years of the Hoover administration in the United Sates (1929–33), despite the reassurances of neoclassical economists that a free market economy unfettered by government interference would soon right itself, the economic situation continually deteriorated, the economy being apparently unable to turn the proverbial corner. American farmers and businessmen found that whatever they produced, the resulting goods merely glutted the market forcing down prices to unprofitable levels. There was the paradox that people living in large cities such as New York in the 1930s were going hungry, while not 50 miles away on Long Island, farmers were ploughing under crops and new-born piglets because bringing them to market would merely involve additional losses.

These depressing economic occurrences were inconsistent with Say's Law and neoclassical theory. The fact that industries were firing workers, and therefore swelling the ranks of the unemployed was theoretically impossible and therefore inconceivable to the neoclassical economic 'experts' of the day. The facts of the Great Depression just did not fit orthodox theory.

Faced with the appalling evidence of rising unemployment and continual business losses during the last three years of the Hoover administration, neoclassical economic theorists grudgingly admitted that temporary departures from full employment were possible, just as a swinging pendulum might temporarily move away from its equilibrium position of rest. But, like the free swinging pendulum, the economy, if left alone, would quickly right itself. President Herbert Hoover, listening to the conservative neoclassical economic experts of his day, was paralysed into inaction. He could only promise that if government remained neutral and allowed free enterprise to go about its business 'prosperity was right around the corner'. The economy would right itself in the long run.

But things just went from bad to worse during the years of the Hoover administration. By the 1932 election, people were in such desperate straits that it was feared that they might turn to another economic system – maybe fascism, socialism, or even communism – in the hopes of improving the economic situation. Fear and the political rumblings of a possible upheaval reverberated throughout the USA. It was no longer politically feasible to wait for the neoclassical 'long run' when the economy was supposed to right itself. Prosperity was not around the corner – revolution and anarchy was!

Before the end of the Hoover administration, an army of thousands of unemployed veterans of the First World War marched on Washington to demand that something be done and set up a tent city near the Potomac River in Washington while waiting for government action. The media labelled the tent city – and others that grew up around the country – 'Hoovervilles'. Fearing violence, President Hoover called in the army under General Douglas MacArthur to destroy the Hooverville in Washington and to disperse the veterans. The general did not hesitate to use extreme force to achieve these objectives.

In 1932, in accepting the nomination for the President, Franklin Delano Roosevelt, noting the long-term devastated state of the US economy since 1929, told the Democratic Convention: 'I pledge you – and I pledge myself – to a new deal for the American people'.

Roosevelt easily defeated Hoover in the November election as the American people desperately sought a 'new deal' from the economic deck. Roosevelt, however, did not take office until March of 1933. By then, the US economy was in complete shambles. People feared the future. In his inaugural address on 4 March 1933 Roosevelt told the nation: 'Let me assert my firm belief that the only thing we have to fear is fear itself.'

Roosevelt realized that the economic experts of the day had been unable to provide any useful advice for his predecessor and that, unless some improvement was obtained soon, the existing capitalist system was unlikely to survive. Instead of continuing to rely on the 'conventional wisdom' of such experts, Roosevelt recruited a group of intelligent younger people, his 'Brain Trust', and asked them to look for new economic approaches to solve the unemployment problem. The Brain Trust included Rexford Tugwell, an economist, and Adolf A. Berle, a lawyer. In the 1920s Tugwell had freed himself from the analytical yoke of orthodox neoclassical theory, while Berle, since he was trained as a lawyer and not as an economist, had no great attachment to it.

Keynes was, of course, already working on his revolutionary book. By the time of Roosevelt's inauguration in 1933, Keynes had attracted considerable attention to the unorthodox policies which he advocated. In his lectures and published papers during the early 1930s Keynes was developing new ideas for his 'General Theory', and these scattered utterings were given a wide circulation in both Britain and the United States.

The policy suggestions implied in Keynes's writings and speeches provided some rationalization for the large public works programmes that pragmatists, such as Tugwell and Berle, recognized had to be undertaken if people's incomes were to be resuscitated and increased. This increase in people's income – which, in those days was called 'pump-priming' – was thought to be necessary in order to assure entrepreneurs that the markets for their products would revive. This, in turn, would end the moribund expectations of entrepreneurs who, seeing that consumers again had some money in their pockets, would be encouraged to expand production and create additional employment. Thus the economic pump would be primed to provide additional jobs and economic security for all.

The new president was well aware of the precariousness of the situation, and recognized that the electorate would only give him a short time to show that he could get the economy on the move again. Accordingly, Roosevelt quickly instituted his New Deal legislative programme – an odd array of legislative initiatives only some of which incorporated the policy implications Keynes had discussed in his public lectures and articles. Keynes's book, *The General Theory*, which developed the analytical premises upon which his policy suggestions were based, was still three years away from being published.

Under the stimulation of Roosevelt's New Deal, the American economy immediately began to improve. The number of people employed rose from a low of 38.8 million when Roosevelt took office in 1933 to 50.8 million before the Japanese attack on Pearl Harbor in 1941. The per capita real income of the American people grew by 70 per cent in these eight years. By the time the United States entered the Second World War, prosperity had returned to the country. Happy economic days were here again!

The American electorate overwhelmingly associated the economic revival with the activist economic policies of Roosevelt's New Deal, especially when they compared their economic fortunes under the Hoover administration's paralysis and neoclassical *laissez-faire* philosophy. Consequently, the people overwhelmingly re-elected Roosevelt for an unprecedented third term in the election of 1940. For the American people of that time, there was no question that the New Deal (and Keynes's) policies worked!

Although many of the New Deal policies contributed to the recovery, the underlying theory justifying these policies was not published until February 1936 by Keynes in his book, *The General Theory of Employment, Interest and Money*. Keynes felt it was necessary first to dislodge neoclassical economic theory from both the minds of economics experts and their textbooks in order to convince them permanently of the fallacy of Say's Law and the inapplicability of assuming 'neutral money'. Keynes believed that only after the economics profession comprehended a general theory of a monetary production economy would they permanently pressure policy-makers to take positive actions to eliminate unemployment, rather than wait upon the long-run free market to swing to full employment equilibrium.

By 1936, Keynes had worked out, in sufficient detail, the analytical foundations of his 'General Theory' of 'a monetary production economy' where 'money is not neutral'. Unfortunately much of the analysis that Keynes emphasized in *The General Theory* was, in the Cambridge (University) oral tradition, developed in response to discussion of early drafts of Keynes's book by a group of younger colleagues at Cambridge who called themselves 'the circus'. These 'circus' participants included Joan and Austin Robinson, Richard Kahn and James Meade. Accordingly, the emphasized analytical aspects of Keynes' *The General Theory* dealt primarily with those areas which particularly puzzled this particular group. Other theoretical areas, which might have been confusing to outsiders, were apparently clear to these colleagues who had access to oral discussions between Keynes and others at Cambridge. This made the analysis in the book more difficult for those outside of Cambridge to follow.

In the United States the younger economists of that day, some who have since become Nobel Prize winners – such as Paul Samuelson and James Tobin – were well-read in modern mathematics, even as they were nurtured on neoclassical theory. They were therefore less aware of many of the nuances of theoretical analysis which were part of the Cambridge oral tradition. Since the orthodox neoclassical theory that these young American economists were trained in did not provide the relief for the Great Depression, this younger generation was anxious to break the orthodox hold on the thinking of the economics profession championed by the majority of their elders. They cheered and championed Keynes's policies and his book, even though they did not quite understand Keynes's analytical structure.

Without a clear understanding of Keynes's analytical structure, many of the younger generation tried to reconcile the neoclassical theoretical analysis on which they had been weaned with Keynes's policy prescriptions requiring government to take actions to assure full employment rather than rely on market processes.

With few exceptions, the elder generation – the neoclassical establishment of the economics profession in the United States as well as some of Keynes's colleagues in England – did not understand his book but correctly recognized it as a threat to their professed analytical thought in which they had a life-long investment. It is said that one established American economist characterized Keynes's 'General Theory' by saying: 'There are a lot of new things and true things in Mr Keynes's Book. Unfortunately the new is not true and the true is not new.'

Thus, for over a decade following the publication of Keynes's *General Theory*, a controversy raged in the economics profession between the elder neoclassical economists and the mainly younger generation of proponents of Keynesian policies. The elders were experts in neoclassical economics. Recognizing that Keynes's analysis was logically incompatible with their own analytical approach, the elder economists, as an article of faith, decried Keynes's analysis as faulty.

The younger generation had also been nurtured on neoclassical theory. They may have yearned for some action to rid the economy of The Great Depression and may have also wanted to overthrow their elders; but they did not wish entirely to destroy the analytical structure which they had spent so many years in school learning to master. They therefore tried to amalgamate the neoclassical theoretical analysis with Keynes's activist policies (for getting government to control employment, aggregate investment, and price level aspects of the economy) to develop an analytical structure which they grandiosely called Neoclassical Synthesis Keynesianism. This synthesis attempted to integrate Keynes's policies for the twentieth-century economy with the nineteenth-century neoclassical theory which embodied Say's Law and the neutrality of money axiom as long-run propositions. If there were logical inconsistencies in the analysis of this neoclassical synthesis, they were readily obscured in a sea of unhelpful mathematical symbolism. The controversy in the literature eventually ended as the elder generation died out after the Second World War and the younger generation inherited the vacant Establishment positions at the prestigious universities.

Independent of the academic controversy of the 1930s and 1940s, the economic recovery under Roosevelt clearly proved the soundness of Keynes's suggestions for an active governmental role. By the end of the Second World War, although Keynes the man was dead, many in the economics establishment had accepted Keynesian policies – as did policy-makers worldwide. Yet, a major basis for Keynes' theoretical analysis – his rejection of the long-run neutrality of money axiom – had never really become established in the economics profession.

Professor Paul Samuelson at the Massachusetts Institute of Technology and Professor James Tobin at Yale University, became among the best-known academic leaders of the new generation who declared themselves to be 'Keynesians' and who continued to utilize this Neoclassical Synthesis Keynesianism analysis. Since the logic of this synthesis was based on axioms which presumed a long-run non-inflationary full employment outcome for a free market economic system, these 'Keynesians' reduced Keynes's analysis to that of merely providing a 'quick fix' for the short-run disruptions that shocked the economic system. In the long run, despite Keynes's dictum to the contrary, these self-styled Neoclassical Synthesis Keynesians believed that the market would right itself. It was only because the market took too long to make the necessary adjustments that, according to these impatient young neoclassical Keynesians, the system would occasionally need doses of Keynesian medicine.

Keynes, however, had written his analytical scheme in an attempt to overthrow both the short-run *and* the long-run versions of neoclassical theory. He had accused neoclassical economists of:

> ...resembling Euclidean geometers in a non-Euclidean world who, discovering that in experience straight lines apparently parallel often meet, rebuke the lines for not keeping straight – as the only remedy for the unfortunate collisions which are occurring. Yet, in truth there is no remedy except to overthrow the axiom of parallels and to work out a non-Euclidean geometry. Something similar is required to-day in Economics.[2]

That something similar, according to Keynes, was to work out the equivalent of a non-Euclidean economics without the axiom of the neutrality of money. Keynes's analytical framework was therefore logically incompatible with the American Keynesian neoclassical synthesis for the latter maintained the assumption of the neutrality of money – at least for the long run. Keynes's analytical scheme never really got a firm footing in the economic literature. Hence, this American version of Keynesianism captured the post-Second World War economics profession, just as the earlier nineteenth-century neoclassical analysis had, in Keynes's view, '...conquered England as completely as the Holy Inquisition conquered Spain'.[3]

Thus neoclassical theory survived. Since the Keynesian Revolution was thought to be located entirely in the macroeconomics of the aggregate economy, academic discussions of the microeconomics of the individual enterprise still was based on neoclassical principles. By the 1970s neoclassical economics had made a resurgence in popularity – a counter-revolution – among economists. The theoretical foundations of neoclassical economics spread from microeconomic theory (that is, the theory of economic behaviour of individual firms and households) to macroeconomics (the study of the economic behaviour of economic systems). In the 1970s and 1980s, neoclassical theory again dominated economic textbooks and the work of many recent Nobel Prize winners in Economics.

How was this possible? The answer, according to economists who call themselves Post Keynesians, lies partly in the sociology of the economics profession and its development since the 1930s. Especially important was economists' desires to be recognized as members of a 'hard science' discipline, especially compared with their softer social science sisters such as sociology or political science.

The younger generation was well-read in modern mathematics, even as they were nurtured on neoclassical theory. They did not wish to destroy totally the neoclassical structure that they had spent so many years in school learning to master. More importantly, they did not quite understand Keynes's analytical structure. Professor Tobin explains why:

> Keynes did not help them understand his point. In keeping with the ethnoscentrism of English economics, especially at Cambridge, he paid little attention to continental writers.... Keynes used only simple mathematics, and that sparingly. His language, terminology, and style of argument were pragmatic and worldly like Alfred Marshall's rather than rigorous and abstract like Walras's. Although he did in fact set forth a system of simultaneous equations, he did not present them with formal clarity. Most students owe their understanding of it to elucidations by Hicks and others.[4]

At approximately the same time that Keynes was publishing his *General Theory*, neoclassical theory regarding the efficacy of Adam Smith's 'invisible hand' of free market forces was being rewritten via sophisticated mathematical methods into what appeared to be a more rigorous, formal discipline. This mathematized version of neoclassical theory is called General Equilibrium Theory, or Walrasian equilibrium analysis, for it has its antecedents in the works of Leon Walras, a nineteenth-century French economist who developed the first mathematical version of this theory.

The rigour of this mathematical translation of what neoclassical theorists always regarded as the absolute truth permitted economists to claim their discipline was a 'hard science'. Professor Tobin states that this Walrasian approach or

> ... modern general equilibrium theory is the basic paradigm of our discipline, and as it happens, the scientific counterpart of the common central theme of the conservative counter-revolutions, the Invisible Hand.[5]

Tobin continues:

> Where does the modern version of the theory leave the Invisible Hand? Two quite opposite responses are conceivable. On the one hand is the good news: the intuitions of Adam Smith and many later writers can indeed be rigorously formulated and proved. The bad news is that the theorems depend on a host of conditions, many of dubious realism. Restrictions on preferences and technologies are stringent... The theory does not describe a process in real time by which the economy reaches an equilibrium solution.... The modern version might be taken to refute, not to support, the applicability of invisible hand propositions to real world economies.[6]

As we learn about the ongoing debate between neoclassical economists and Post Keynesians, we shall see that economists who use the neoclassical analysis are relying primarily on Tobin's good news; while the Post Keynesians have accentuated the 'bad news'.

The lack of realism associated with the neoclassical treatment of a money concept is particularly important in separating Keynes from the neoclassical approach. Professor Tobin, who won the Nobel Prize for his contributions to developing the monetary aspects of General Equilibrium Theory, states:

> Money has always been an awkward puzzle for neoclassical general equilibrium theory.... The holdings of intrinsically useless paper as a store of value is a puzzle... there is no need for money holdings.... [Yet] common sense tells us money is held and has value....It is not easy to incorporate this common-sense observation in the standard paradigm....The makeshift compromise in neoclassical theory has been the alleged *neutrality* of money.... The application of this neu-

trality proposition to actual real-world monetary policies is a prime example of the fallacy of misplaced concreteness.[7]

Moreover, as Tobin himself points out, 'Keynes rejected the neutrality of money'.[8] Hence there is a clear logical separation on the basis of how to handle the money concept. Despite the belief in the popular media that Keynesian thought has dominated economic theory since the end of the Second World War, it is the neoclassical general equilibrium approach which has attracted the 'best and the brightest' of the economics profession for the last few decades. As Tobin describes the development of this neoclassical general equilibrium analysis:

> ... the task of giving rigour and precision to the relation of individual actions and aggregate outcomes has engaged the best minds of our profession including Walras, Pareto, Hicks, Samuelson, Debreu, and Arrow.[9]

As a result, according to Tobin:

> Many of the ablest minds attracted into professional economics find their exposure to general equilibrium theory the most exciting intellectual experience of their lives. Elegant, rigorous, mathematically powerful, the theory reaches far from obvious results. It gives economics a theoretical core that 'softer' social sciences lack and often envy. It 'is the only game in town'. It especially enchants those who were drawn into the profession more because it challenges their mathematical and logical skills than because it might help to solve real world puzzles and problems.... The patent and admitted unrealism of assumptions does not matter.[10]

Realism, apparently, is not a hallmark for sophisticated economic theory.

Despite the academic controversy that raged during the period 1936–46, the economic recovery under Roosevelt suggested to many politicians that policies based on 'Keynes's Revolution' were sound. By the time the Second World War was over, most of those in the professional Economics establishment accepted Keynesian activist policies even though they did not really grasp his revolutionary theory. Politicians worldwide were receptive to Keynesian policies to avoid depressions rather than rely on the invisible hand, as President Hoover's neoclassical advisors had suggested.

Thus, as we have seen, for neoclassical Keynesians, Keynes's analysis merely implies that it may take time – sometimes a long time – for the free market to provide a full employment economic environment. As Professor Solow stated in 1979:

> Adjustment processes are at best slow; for better or worse, money wages and prices are not very flexible in response to excess suppliers.... In this approach disequilibrium can persist for a long time. A further implication of the same line of thought is that the economy will very likely adapt slowly to external shocks, whether they originate on the demand side or the supply side. Macroeconomic equilibrium is thus vulnerable to all sorts of disturbances.[11]

Keynes, however, believed that no matter how long the time period was, a market economy may not possess adjusting mechanisms to correct the system. As we have seen, by 1933 Keynes had clearly distinguished between the neoclassical views of his day and the 'General Theory' he was working on, in terms of whether or not money could be presumed neutral. Hence, according to the Post Keynesians, Tobin's makeshift compromise of the neutrality of money is logically incompatible with Keynes's analysis.

NOTES

1. J. M. Keynes, 'A Monetary Theory of Production' in *The Collected Writings of John Maynard Keynes*, vol. XIII, Macmillan, London, 1971, p. 409 (some emphases added).
2. J. M. Keynes, *The General Theory of Employment, Interest and Money*, Harcourt Brace, New York, 1936, p. 16.
3. Ibid., p. 32.
4. J. Tobin, 'Theoretical Issues in Macroeconomics' in G. R. Feiwel (ed.), *Issues in Contemporary Macroeconomics and Distribution*, State University of New York Press, Albany, 1985, p. 110.
5. Tobin, op. cit., p. 104.

6. Ibid., p. 106.
7. Ibid., op. cit., pp. 108–9.
8. Ibid., p. 113.
9. Ibid., p. 105.
10. Ibid., p. 105.
11. R. M. Solow, 'Alternative Approaches to Macroeconomics', *Canadian Journal of Economics*, 1976, p. 345.

3. Post Keynesianism: a Reaction to American 'Keynesians'

In Britain after the Second World War, some of Keynes's students and followers still occupied important academic positions. These included Sir Roy Harrod of Oxford University and Cambridge professors Joan Robinson, Lord Richard Kahn and Lord Nicholas Kaldor. These English followers of Keynes explicitly argued that what had developed in the United States as Keynesian theory – the neoclassical synthesis – was not what Keynes had written about in his 'General Theory'.

Professor Joan Robinson noted that Keynes's proposed revolution in economics was on both the plane of theory and on the plane of policy. She wrote:

> On the plane of theory the main point of the 'General Theory' was to break out of the cocoon of equilibrium and consider the nature of life lived in time, the difference between yesterday and tomorrow, here and now, the past is irrevocable and the future is unknown. This was too great a shock. Orthodox [neoclassical] theory managed to wind up into a cocoon again. Keynes had shown how money is a necessary feature of an economy in which the future's uncertain and he showed what part monetary and financial institutions play in the functioning of the real economy....In the Keynesian theory after the war this simple point is lost. The whole of Keynes' argument is put to sleep. Keynes is smothered and orthodox equilibrium theory is enthroned once more. Keynes was writing and arguing against the prevailing orthodoxy. He had to argue first and last that something could be done.[1]

Thus, those followers of Keynes who knew him at Cambridge while he was struggling to develop his analytical framework, argued that what passed for Keynesian economics after the Second

World War was far from the theoretical analysis that Keynes had presented. Indeed, Joan Robinson labelled the American Neoclassical Synthesis Keynesianism 'Bastard Keynesianism'. But, like Keynes, these English economists followed the English tradition of arguing pragmatically and sparingly, using only the simplest mathematics. Consequently, their words fell on the deaf ears of the mathematically trained American economists who believed themselves scientifically superior because of their ability to manipulate complicated mathematical symbols. In response to this so-called scientific superiority based on the use of mathematics, Joan Robinson is said to have exclaimed, 'I never learned to use mathematics to develop theory; therefore I had to learn how to *think* about problems'. Nevertheless, Joan Robinson recognized that the American version of Keynesianism was gaining the upper hand in academic circles.

> The doctrines of the new era have been attributed to Keynes, but the dominant economic theory of the time in North American and spreading from there over the world, is what I have called the 'Bastard Keynesian doctrine'. I do not use this term just as abuse. It has a definite meaning. The old orthodoxy against which the Keynesian revolution was raised was based on Say's Law, there cannot be deficiency of demand. The Bastard Keynesian doctrine has allowed all the old doctrines to creep back in again. Keynes was diagnosing a defect inherent in capitalism. But the Bastard Keynesians turned the argument back into a defense of laissez-faire. The old orthodoxy of laissez-faire, against which the Keynesian Revolution was raised, taught that the free play of free market forces could be relied upon to establish equilibrium with full employment.[2]

The Neoclassical Synthesis Keynesianism taught that temporary or short-run lapses from full employment could be offset by means of government policy. Simultaneously, this school of economic thought reiterated the doctrines of *laissez-faire* and the long-run adulation of the free market economy. The general moral of their song was that economists now understood how to develop governmental policies to alleviate short-run, temporary unemployment episodes, and hence there could be a perpetually growing free market economy in harmony and contentment.

The stage was set for a new debate in economics between the American School and the staunch defenders of Keynes's revolutionary analytical system. The latter group of scholars believed that they understood the true heretical nature of Keynes's approach and wanted to continue to develop Keynes's revolutionary system. Besides the English contingent, in the 1950s in the United States only Professor Sidney Weintraub of the University of Pennsylvania laboured to revive interest in Keynes's original General Theory analytical approach. Beginning in the 1960s, his efforts were buttressed by the work of his former student, Professor Paul Davidson.

Although these economists on both sides of the Atlantic objected to the neoclassical synthesis, they were far from an organized group during this early period. It was not until the 1970s that these various writers coalesced around some common analytical principles and procedures. They then became formally known as Post Keynesians.

From the very beginning these Post Keynesians insisted that the American Neoclassical Synthesis Keynesians had never fully understood the revolutionary analysis of Keynes's 'General Theory'. American Neoclassical Synthesis Keynesians developed a mongrel, or bastardized, approach to Keynesian theory which, the Post Keynesians claimed, would lead to theoretical and policy errors as new and different problems developed in the postwar economy.

Most Neoclassical Synthesis Keynesians only grudgingly admitted the plausibility of the Post Keynesian criticisms; they did not admit the possibility that the original Keynes approach might prove more fruitful. Professor James Tobin has written:

A school of self-styled post-Keynesians regard any synthesis or reconciliation, in substance or in language, of Keynes and neoclassical economics, as a betrayal of the revolution. They reject equilibrium analysis altogether, stress the historical, institutional, and evolutionary aspects of economic development, and emphasize the macroeconomic implications of the non-competitive structure of modern economies. Their valid points do not add up to a coherent theory.[3]

In a myriad of books and articles beginning with Professor Sidney Weintraub's 1958 classic *An Approach to the Theory of Income Distribution*, his 1956 article on 'A Macroeconomic Approach to the Theory of Wages' in the *American Economic Review* and 1957 article on 'The Microfoundations of Aggregate Demand and Supply' in the *Economic Journal*, American Post Keynesians continued to drum away at the differences between Keynes's analysis and the neoclassical synthesis of 'Bastard Keynesianism'. It took many years before their work had any significant influence on the direction of economic analysis, but by the end of the 1960s, the resurgence of inflation – and the inability of the Neoclassical Synthesis Keynesians to provide a solution – attracted some inquisitive minds towards the Post Keynesian analysis, which did have a policy solution that seemed to work in countries such as Holland, Austria and elsewhere, when consistently and pragmatically applied. This Post Keynesian policy was labelled an 'incomes policy' and is described further in Chapter 9.

It was more than likely that it was the inability of the American Keynesians to deal with inflation rather than any cogent analytical criticisms of neoclassical Keynesianism by the Post Keynesians which created interest in the Post Keynesian approach. The vast majority of economists tend not to question existing orthodoxy during periods of relatively satisfactory economic performance in real-world economies – even when the orthodox analysis is shown to be logically faulty and/or unrealistic. Only in periods of economic crisis will a significant number (but even then not necessarily a majority) of economists search for new, more relevant theoretical approaches for analysing economic problems. The Post Keynesian alternative to neoclassical theory, therefore, would have to wait for a real-life economic crisis before it could attract many converts.

With the surge of inflation at the end of the 1960s and its acceleration in the 1970s, coupled with the inability of neoclassical Keynesian theory to develop a successful anti-inflation policy, some economists moved towards a more Post Keynesian approach, while others moved towards a pure, less hybrid, neoclassical approach known as monetarism. The latter rejected any synthesis with Keynesian views.

One of the more important converts to the Post Keynesian approach was Sir John Hicks who would win the Nobel Prize in Economics in 1972 for his fundamental contribution to the development of Neoclassical Synthesis Keynesianism. In 1937, Hicks, as a young economist at the London School of Economics, had been heavily influenced by the continental neoclassical economists, among them the Austrian Frederick von Hayek who was on the Faculty of the London School at the time. Hayek, a contemporary of Keynes, had been one of the leading exponents of orthodox neoclassical theory in England. Scattered references to Hayek, in Keynes's *The General Theory*, indicate that Keynes used Hayek's ideas to illustrate particular errors in the neoclassical scheme.

Young Hicks, well versed in mathematics and foreign languages, developed the nineteenth-century neoclassical analysis of the French economist, Leon Walras, into a mathematical piece of analysis which he claimed could embody Keynes's method – Hicks' analysis was called the IS–LM system. This IS–LM label was applied because it was believed that the Hicks' system summarized the four basic pillars of Keynes's 'General Theory': I for investment, S for savings, L for the demand for liquidity, and M for the supply of money. Hicks suggested that his IS–LM formalization provided the mathematical basis for integrating Keynes's *General Theory* with the works of Walras. Since the latter had not been translated into English and hence was virtually unread, Hicks's claim was readily accepted. Thus, Hicks, like James Mill a century earlier, gave a particular importance to the writings of an obscure Frenchman. This Hicksian structure of simultaneous equations claimed to set out Keynes's General Theory with formal clarity. In his book, *Value and Capital*, Hicks claimed:

> I believe I had the fortune to come upon a method of analysis which is applicable to a wide variety of economic problems.... The method of General Equilibrium...was specially designed to exhibit the economic system as a whole.... We shall thus be able to see just why it is that Mr. Keynes reaches different results from earlier economists on crucial matters of social policy.[4]

American Keynesians immediately seized upon Hicks's IS–LM apparatus, based on Walras' general equilibrium approach, and used it as the foundation of their own neoclassical synthesis. Students were told that they did not have to read Keynes's difficult and tedious *General Theory*, but could study instead the IS–LM system which their professors assured them encapsulated all of Keynes's important ideas. As Professor Tobin has already told us, most students today owe their understanding of the Keynesian analysis to the elucidation of Hicks. Indeed, the mathematical apparatus developed by Hicks became a universal truth for most American economists, so much so that 30 years later it is alleged that Professor Martin Bronfenbrenner of Duke University referred to the Hicksian apparatus as 'the ISLAMic religion of economists'.

With his IS–LM equational system, the young Hicks of the 1930s became a forefather of what Joan Robinson would call 'Bastard Keynesianism'. In the mid-1970s, however, this Hicksian equational system failed to provide any workable solution to the inflation problem plaguing the free world. Hicks – now Sir John Hicks, a Nobel Prize winner – apparently recognized the errant ways of his neoclassical youth, writing in 1976:

> The Keynesian Revolution went off at half-cock. These equilibrists did not know that they were beaten... they thought that what Keynes had said could be absorbed into their equilibrium system; all that was needed was that the scope of their equilibrium system should be extended. As we know, there has been a lot of extension, a vast amount of extension, what I am saying is that it has never quite got to the point... to look over my own work, since 1935, and to show how some aspects of the struggle, and the muddle, are reflected in it ... I have found myself facing the same issue, and (very often) being baffled by it.[5]

And by 1977, Hicks wrote of the work for which he had been awarded the Nobel Prize:

> This is work which has become part of the standard literature of what is called in modern controversy 'neoclassical economics'. But it was done a long time ago, and it was with mixed feelings that I found myself honoured for that work, which I felt myself to have outgrown.

In spite of all that has since happened to that particular piece of theory – the further elaborations at the hands of Samuelson, of Debreu, of so many others – the time came when I felt that I had done with it.

I could see that it was nonsense. It does deliberate violence to the *order* in which the real world (in *any* real world) events occur.

It was this formal model of Keynes which I summarized in the ISLM diagram. There is indeed much more in the *General Theory* of Keynes than this formal model, and very much more in some of Keynes's other writings, which can be quite properly used to elucidate his work.[6]

By the winter of 1980–81, Hicks's conversion away from neoclassical economics towards a Post Keynesian analytical approach was complete. He wrote in the *Journal of Post Keynesian Economics:*

The IS-LM diagram, which is widely, but not universally, accepted as a convenient synopsis of Keynesian theory, is a thing for which I can not deny that I have some responsibility. It first saw light in a paper of my own, 'Mr. Keynes and the Classics' (1937) but it was actually written for a meeting of the Econometric Society in Oxford in September 1936, just eight months after the publication of *The General Theory....* I have, however, not concealed that, as time has gone on, I have myself become dissatisfied with it.[7]

With these dramatic confessions and recantations by Hicks, it is easier to understand the complaints by the Post Keynesians that so-called Keynesian theory was subverted onto a wrong track by the Neoclassical Synthesis Keynesian analysis. In the early 1970s, even James Tobin, a founder of the American neoclassical synthesis school, expressed doubt as to its antecedents when he wrote:

I do not know what to call those of us who take an eclectic...view. 'Neo-Keynesian' will do, I guess, but so would 'neoclassical'. The synthesis of the last twenty-five years certainly contains many elements not in the *General Theory*. Perhaps it should be called Hicksian, since it derives... from his IS–LM article.[8]

Yet despite all the benefits of hindsight, and the admission of some of the leaders of the Neoclassical Synthesis Keynesian school of economic thought that their model does not accurately reflect Keynes's revolutionary analysis, the dispute between these neoclassical 'Keynesians' and the Post Keynesians regarding the proper analytical model for comprehending real-world economic problems has continued – with dramatic implications for public economic policy. And some of the fundamental issues dividing these economists remain. Moreover, the failure of Neoclassical Synthesis Keynesian theory to provide workable policy prescriptions for the pressing problems of the 1970s – simultaneous inflation and stagnation of the economy, better known as stagflation – has permitted other schools of thought, such as monetarism, to gain the public spotlight. To understand these conflicting views, we must pursue a deeper investigation of the implications of the differences in emphasis and policy prescriptions between the Post Keynesian school and neoclassical economists and other schools of economic thought.

NOTES

1. J. Robinson, *Collected Economic Papers*, V, MIT Press, Boston, 1980, p. 121.
2. J. Robinson, *Collected Economic Papers*, V, op. cit., p. 121.
3. J. Tobin, 'Theoretical Issues in Macroeconomics' in G. R. Feiwel (ed.), *Issues in Contemporary Macroeconomics and Distribution*, State University of New York Press, Albany, 1985, p. 115.
4. J. R. Hicks, *Value and Capital*, Oxford University Press, Oxford, 1939, p. 4.
5. J. R. Hicks, 'Some Questions of Time In Economics' in A. M. Tang *et al.* (eds), *Evolution, Welfare and Time in Economics*, Lexington Books, Massachusetts, 1976, pp. 140–1.
6. J. R. Hicks, *Economic Perspectives*, Oxford University Press, Oxford, 1977, pp. v–vi.
7. J. R. Hicks, 'ISLM – An Explanation', *Journal of Post Keynesian Economics*, **3**, p. 139.
8. J. Tobin, 'Friedman's Theoretical Framework' in R. A. Gordon (ed.), *Milton Friedman's Monetary Framework: A Debate With His Critics*, University of Chicago Press, Chicago, 1974, p. 77.

4. The Analysis of an Uncertain Future

Most economists recognize that all theories are abstractions and therefore simplifications of reality. But the purpose of theory should be to make the real world intelligible, rather than to substitute an ideal theoretical world remote from the facts of experience in order to make the analysis easily tractable.

Professor Milton Friedman, on the other hand, in outlining his 'Methodology of Positive Economics', has apparently convinced many that the lack of reality underlying the fundamental characteristics of one's economic model are not important. He has argued that a theory must abstract from the

> ...mass of complex and detailed circumstances surrounding the phenomena to be explained....To be important *a hypothesis must be descriptively false in its assumptions*.... [T]he relevant question to ask about the 'assumptions' of a theory is not whether they are descriptively 'realistic', for they never are, but whether they are sufficiently good approximations for the purpose in hand. And this question can be answered only by seeing whether the theory works, which means it yields sufficiently accurate predictions.[1]

For Friedman and the many followers of his 'positive economics' methodology, the unquestioning acceptance of delusive axioms and simplifications are essential elements in constructing any useful economic theory. The only valid test of the usefulness of any economic theory is whether it provides accurate predictions regarding future outcomes. Moreover, in Friedman's view, accurate predictions regarding the 'long run' are all that matter. In the belief that his unrealistic theoretical framework for monetary analysis is appropriate, he states:

We have accepted the quantity theory presumption, and have thought it supported by the evidence we examined, that changes in the quantity of money as such *in the long run* have a negligible effect on real income, so that nonmonetary forces are 'all that matter' for real income over decades and 'money does not matter'.[2]

In other words, the long-run neutrality of money is a fundamental presumption of Friedman's monetarist analysis.

Friedman's conception of the length of this long run, however, remains ill-defined. He does not suggest how many weeks, years or decades are required to make up a long run. Does it encompass two years or two decades, or 20, or 200? Unless a well specified length of calendar time is defined as the long run, it will be unclear as to how much evidence must be compiled before one can either reject or accept the idea that there is an agreement between the theory's long-run prediction and the facts of experience. Whenever the predictions of Friedman's analysis are not compatible with the facts over any particular length of calendar time, one can always rationalize this apparent lack of confluence between fact and theory as not yet being in 'the long run'.

In contradistinction to Friedman's view that all that is important is the predictability of *long-run* outcomes by theory, no matter how unrealistic the assumptions, Keynes's argument that 'In the *long run* we are all dead' meant that he believed the focus of economic analysis had to be on immediate remedies for impending real-world problems.

> ...this *long run* is a misleading guide to current affairs. *In the long run* we are all dead. Economists set themselves too easy, too useless a task if in tempestuous seasons they can only tell us that when the storm is long past the ocean is flat again.[3]

Accordingly, we have a fundamental philosophical difference between Keynes and his Post Keynesian followers and neoclassical economists who accept some version of Friedman's test of predictability as the sole basis for the acceptability of a theory.

Friedman insists that the dubious basis of fundamental assumptions is irrelevant. He readily boasts that the axioms underlying his neoclassical analysis are unrealistic. Nevertheless he justifies its use for *practical* policy problems by arguing that a good analysis should presume that individuals and firms, in Friedman's terms, 'behave *as if*' they lived in the world that neoclassical theory describes – even though it represents a fanciful description of the world we humans inhabit.

In the eyes of proponents such as Friedman, the virtue of neoclassical analysis is its ability to predict precise and unique outcomes, even if these results are not likely to occur except in the very long run – when we are all dead.

Post Keynesians, on the other hand, have argued that neoclassical models, including the American Neoclassical Synthesis Keynesian system, abstract from precisely those features that make the real world real. In the Post Keynesian view, economic decisions are made by human beings facing an uncertain and unpredictable economic future, while they are moving away from a fixed and *irreversible past*. Human beings recognize that they have made errors in the past, and that when one makes errors, one has to live with their consequences.

Post Keynesians emphasize the fallibility of human nature and the fact that unfettered human economic decisions do not necessarily automatically result in the best of all possible worlds. The developing economic system is an evolutionary processes where human expectations regarding an uncertain and an unpredictable future will have unavoidable and significant effects on economic outcomes.

In the context of this evolving economy, economic and political institutions play a significant role in shaping expectations about the otherwise unforeseeable future. Decisions based on these sensible expectations *create* a path along which the economy travels. Post Keynesians believe, therefore, that human beings have the power to create and control their own economic destiny. They do not have to accept future economic events as the inevitable consequences of some natural law. This Post Keynesian view that economic theory must stress evolution and institutions in a historical setting has led one leading Neoclassical Synthesis

Keynesian, Yale Professor James Tobin, to characterize Post Keynesians in the following terms:

> They reject equilibrium analysis altogether, stress the historical, institutional, and evolutionary aspects of economic development. [4]

The neoclassical economic theory of monetarists such as Professor Friedman and Neoclassical Synthesis Keynesians such as Professor Tobin, on the other hand, asserts that long-run economic behaviour follows immutable rules which are sometimes called economic laws – for example, Say's Law. Neoclassical theories are a little like breakfast cereals which, although they come in a wide variety of brand names and pretty packages, are all based on the same fundamental contents. Thus whether neoclassical theories are labelled Walrasian general equilibrium models, Arrow–Debreu systems, rational expectations theory, Neoclassical Synthesis Keynesianism, monetarism or chaos theory, they all share the same fundamental building blocks such as the neutrality of money axiom.

All neoclassical theories presume that the economic system resembles the mechanical systems analysed by nineteenth-century physical scientists. The movement over time of such systems is determined by events and laws existing at the initial instant of time. A presumption of neoclassical theories is that the future path of the economy is already predetermined by the conditions exhibited at the initial instant.

This neoclassical 'initial instant' concept is equivalent to the 'Big Bang' view of the creation. In this 'Big Bang' conceptualization the future paths of all the heavenly bodies are determined in this initial and unique heavenly explosion and, consequently, the future position of any star or planet is predictable. By analogy, therefore, the future position of the economy is, in principle, already known or knowable by individuals analysing market signals. Thus when neoclassical theorists describe people as having 'rational expectations' or 'being able fully to anticipate' the future, they are reasoning via this astronomical analogy.

So long as one believes that the universe is comparable to a mechanical system and obeys immutable laws, then, according to mathematician Alan Turing, the existence of a calculable future can be demonstrated. Turing, an English mathematician, is best known to the layperson for cracking the Germans' 'Enigma Code' during the Second World War. But, as a professional mathematician, he is famous for discovering the Turing machine, a hypothetical device for performing any mathematical calculation that is amenable to the application of immutable rules. Turing demonstrated that if Nature *always* conforms to immutable mathematical laws or rules, then whether human intuition knows these laws or not, the future is conceptually predictable via the use of a Turing machine. Since the motion of the heavenly bodies apparently follow the immutable law of gravity which man has discovered, Turing's argument about the predictability of the future positions of the heavenly bodies is generally accepted.

Neoclassical economists, however, make the quantum leap that if economics is to be a hard science similar to astronomy (or physics), it too must be subject to immutable rules or laws, and hence its future position is predictable by use of a Turing machine. Neoclassical economists claim to have already discovered and developed a complete set of exclusive immutable economic laws and consequently believe that the only remaining purpose of economic research is to analyse existing data to estimate the quantitative parameters necessary to predict *à la* Turing machine.

For Post Keynesians, on the other hand, this belief in a calculable future where the power of statistical laws of probability can be utilized to forecast future economic events seriously underestimates the role and importance of human error and ignorance of the future. Post Keynesians argue that neoclassicism has shunted economists' research off on to a wrong track in a delusive search for immutable quantitative relationships which permit precise predictions regarding future economic outcomes. This desire to forecast the future accurately, which Friedman has made the *sine qua non* of economics, is, in the eyes of Post Keynesians, a search for a Holy Grail of economics which cannot exist. In a letter to R. F. Harrod, dated 4 July 1938 Keynes wrote: '...economics is essentially a moral science and not a natural one'[5] – that is, the predictive capability of the natural sciences is not applicable to economics.

In the real world, many economic actions taken today will involve outcomes far in the future. The elapse of calendar time between decision and outcome is a fundamental fact of experience. The time between the decision to produce and the appearance of the product may take weeks, months or even years. The time between purchasing a capital good or a consumer durable and its being used up while yielding profits or utility is usually measured in years, if not decades. Economic decisions involving the purchase and use of capital and/or consumer durables must be based on far-reaching, forward-looking expectations. The benefits resulting from such spending decisions will depend on events that will occur long after the commitment to economic action has been undertaken.

For example, the decision by a developer to build a condominium apartment complex today must be based on what the developer thinks the profitability of this project will be three years from today – when the complex is finished and the apartments are available for sale and occupancy. The profitability of such a condominium project will depend not only on the current costs of land, but also on the costs of construction over the next three years. It will also depend on the developer's expectations of the demand for such apartments in the specific geographic location of the building site, the tax laws existing at the time of sales, the availability of mortgages, the condition of the neighbourhood, and so on.

Our knowledge about economic events occurring through time is, however, asymmetric: although we may know the past, we cannot be sure that we have any reliable knowledge about the economic future. The future remains to be created by human actions and is not merely determined by some immutable economic law. In other words, for many important economic activities – especially long-duration ones – information about future current outcomes does *not* currently exist. The economic future is yet to be created and is not predetermined by existing rules or economic laws. Accordingly, this future is not computable by any conceivable Turing machine. Yet economic decisions taken today require actions whose consequences cannot, and will not, be known until some future date. The decision-maker must therefore often reach a determination as to what course of action to take (or avoid) without being able reliably to calculate the costs and benefits of such an action. Post Keynesians believe that economic theory should reflect the uncertainty that decision-makers have to deal with in the real world. Sir John Hicks has argued that economic models must reflect that people 'do not know what is going to happen and know that they do not know just what is going to happen. As in history!'[6]

How do neoclassical economists handle the obvious fact that economic decision-makers 'know' that they do not know the uncertain future? They usually finesse the problem by presuming the future is already determined by immutable scientific laws that have existed since the initial instant of the formation of the economy. Consequently, our hypothetical real estate developer already knows (via the operation of a *deus ex [Turing] machina*) how many apartments can be sold in the next three years at any given price *before* she begins the production process.

In those neoclassical models known as Arrow–Debreu models, a Walrasian auctioneer is the Turing machine which provides the developer with information regarding the demand for apartments by costlessly compiling all the orders that buyers place for housing at the initial instant of time for every year into the future. More generally, following Professor Friedman's prescriptions for a 'positive economics', some neoclassical economists presume that even if the developer does not 'know' the demand for apartments three years hence, he will act 'as if' there is a *deus ex machina* which makes sufficient information available regarding orders for future apartments to determine whether or not the project will be profitable.

One variant of this Turing machine approach of neoclassical economists presumes that condominium developers possess 'rational expectations' regarding the future. These rational expectations are formed on the basis that past data on condominium apartment demand provides a perfect statistical guideline for understanding what is going to happen in the future. Hence, the future can be fully anticipated without any persistent error by studying history. In other words, neoclassical economists who utilize 'rational expectations' models believe that the precise mathematical odds for the profitable sales of apartments in any condominium projects already exist and are available to anyone who is willing to make the effort to learn the odds. Future market demand is merely a statistical reflection of the past. Real estate developers and their bankers can, on average, calculate the 'correct' decisions regarding the allocation of resources towards providing real estate development by studying past economic events.

For example, Professors Robert Lucas and Thomas Sargent, have argued that neoclassical theory deals

> ...with various aspects of the general problem of drawing inferences about future behavior from observed economic time series....The belief in the possibility of a nonexperimental empirical economics is equivalent to the belief that inferences of this kind can be made.... If so we can construct a robot decision maker, or model, confront it, theoretically, with various environments and trace out its responses.[7]

Since real estate development is a recurrent economic activity, neoclassical theory is relying on a form of Social Darwinism to justify its assertions regarding developers' abilities correctly to forecast the future. Those developers whose expectations are not rational, it is implied, are doomed to make persistent errors and hence – like the dinosaurs – to perish in a free market environment. This variant of neoclassical theory presumes that the fittest who survive in a free market environment have properly programmed intuitions to act 'as if' they knew the future when they formed their statistically correct 'rational expectations'. Economic decision-making is reduced to the equivalent of playing at the craps table. Economists can, in the words of Lucas and Sargent, think of managers as 'robot decision makers'.

On the other hand, Keynes, who had written an important *Treatise on Probability* early in his career, argued that the economic future was uncertain. Decision-makers, according to Keynes, had no basis for calculating the mathematical odds of success or failure, since history was not a reliable guide for predicting future events. According to Keynes:

> The outstanding fact is the extreme precariousness of the basis of knowledge on which our estimates of prospective yields have to be made. Our knowledge of the factors which will govern the yield on an investment some years hence is usually very slight and often negligible. If we speak frankly, we have to admit that our basis of knowledge for estimating the yield ten years hence of a railway, a copper mine, a textile factory, the goodwill of a patent medicine, an Atlantic liner, a building in the City of London amounts to little and sometimes nothing; or even five years hence. In fact, those who seriously attempt to make any such estimate are often so much in the minority that their behaviour does not govern the market.[8]

Spending on investment projects creates jobs and income which can then be used by the workers to buy the products of other industries. Keynes believed that an entrepreneurial spirit willing to undertake long-lived investment expenditures, in the face of an uncertain future, was a necessary condition for prosperity in a money-using production economy. When investment spending declines, the economy decays, workers lose jobs, factories and stores are boarded up, and the economy collapses.

Keynes argued that, to understand the causes of periods of prosperity and depression, one had to understand the factors that influence businessmen's decisions either to invest or alternatively increase their liquidity position. Unlike the neoclassical theorists, Keynes did not think that investment decisions were based on rationally calculating the 'odds' in a statistically reliable manner based on past observations. He believed that investments were often based on businessmen's optimism or pessimism – in other words, they are based on emotion and an entrepreneurial culture rather than precise calculation. Keynes wrote:

> ...there is the instability due to the characteristic of human nature that a large portion of our positive activities depend on a spontaneous optimism rather than on mathematical expectation.... Most, probably, of our decisions to do something positive, the full consequences of

which will be drawn out over many days to come, can only be taken as the result of animal spirits – of a spontaneous urge to action rather than inaction, and not as the outcome of a weighted average of quantitative benefits multiplied by quantitative probabilities. Enterprise only pretends to itself to be mainly actuated by the statements in its own prospectus, however candid and sincere. Only a little more than an expedition to the South Pole, is it based on an exact calculation of benefits to come. Thus if the animal spirits are dimmed and the spontaneous optimism falters, leaving us to depend on nothing but a mathematical expectation, enterprise will fade and die; though fears of loss may have a basis no more reasonable than hopes of profit had before.... We should not conclude from this that everything depends on waves of irrational psychology....We are merely reminding ourselves that human decisions affecting the future, whether personal or political or economic, cannot depend on strict mathematical expectation, since the basis for making such calculation does not exist; and that it is our innate urge to activity which makes the wheels go round.[9]

With this statement, Keynes denies the basis for modelling investment decisions 'as if' investors were Turing machines. For as long as 'the basis for making such calculations does not exist', a Turing machine is incapable of predicting the future in the short run, the long run, or in any other run. Unlike neoclassical economists who believe that managers behave strictly in accordance with their specific and correct 'rationally' calculated expectations of future profits and losses in deciding whether to engage in investment activities, Post Keynesians have developed Keynes's analysis on the basis of his 'animal spirits' argument. Many crucial investment decisions are undertaken in an atmosphere of uncertainty by those who realize that they cannot possess a knowledge of the odds of success or failure in an economic endeavour which will only bear fruit in the far distant future.

Investment and other important economic decisions which affect employment, economic growth and price stability or instability are, in the Post Keynesian view, dominated by crucial managerial decisions based on expectations regarding an uncertain future. Such decisions are not undertaken by robots who are capable of possessing an actuarial predictable knowledge of success or failure. Recognition that there are no determinable odds for forecasting future profits and losses leads to the inevitable conclusion that there are no constants in economics comparable to the gravitational constant in physics. Economics is unlike physics in that there are no universal immutable rules and laws which govern all possible future economic outcomes.

Accordingly, economics can never resemble the 'hard sciences', and the predictions of economists – unlike those of physicists – cannot always be presented with statistical reliability. While the physicist can confidently predict how rapidly a body will fall if it is tossed off the Leaning Tower of Pisa, a businessman, or his 'expert' economic adviser, can never predict with any assurance how fast or far market demand will fall, or rise, in the future.

From this Keynesian perspective of uncertainty, decision-makers may often either avoid choosing between 'real' alternatives because they 'haven't got a clue' about the future, or they may follow their 'animal spirits' for positive action in a 'damn the torpedoes, full speed ahead' approach. In an uncertain environment, the Keynesian perspective recognizes that human economic behaviour may involve either:

a) 'waiting' – that is, the desire for liquidity, *even in the long run*, so as to avoid committing any earned claims on real resources[10] between choices A or B; and/or
b) 'animal spirits' decisions involving spontaneous and often apparently an arbitrary choice of investments – that is, the chosen investment would appear to be irrational if unchanging probabilities governed *all* future consequences.

In other words, 'irrational' demands for liquidity and/or investments are humanly possible. Such demands involve understandable behaviour in a world where uncertainty and human ignorance of the future is distinguished from probabilistic concepts.

In 1979, as he moved from his earlier neoclassical beliefs towards a Post Keynesian philosophy, Sir John Hicks explained that economic outcomes are not determined by natural forces (natural laws) independent of human action and control:

Economics is in time, in a way that the natural sciences are not. All economic data are dated; so that inductive evidence can never do more than establish a relation which appears to hold within a period to which the data refer. If a relation held ... over (say) the last fifty years... we cannot even reasonably guess it will continue to hold for the next fifty years. In the sciences such guesses are reasonable; in economics they are not. Economics... is on the edge of science and on the edge of history.[11]

For Keynes, and for the Post Keynesians, an uncertain future is significantly different from the neoclassical vision that the future is risky but statistically predictable. Professor Paul Davidson, editor of the *Journal of Post Keynesian Economics*, relates how he tried to confront a famous Neoclassical Synthesis Keynesian with this problem. Davidson wrote:

Recently, when I wrote to Nobel Prize winner Kenneth J. Arrow that Keynes's theory was at variance with general equilibrium theory, he responded 'I am not yet convinced that the distinction between uncertainty and risk is really vital.... The problem in all this is to create something which is genuine theory, that is, a well articulated framework with implications. It is interesting that the parts of Keynesian theory that became popular were, as you suggest, a retrogression from Keynes's deeper insights; but this is no accident. One part of the theory was in fact capable of development even though it was an impoverished version of the whole; the other part, deeper though it was, could not in fact be developed.'[12]

Davidson then added, 'I would hope that even prize-winning theorists will realize that economists need not accept retrogression as development'.[13]

Post Keynesians believe that it is necessary to study the evolving economic institutions and processes over time to explain what is happening. Except for humdrum routine economic decisions, it is unlikely that the future can be reliably predicted on the basis of past evidence or even current events. For many important economic decisions, especially those involving the accumulation of wealth, it is not useful to try to predict precisely – and possibly incorrectly – what will happen in the future on the basis of past events. Because Post Keynesians do not believe that there are timeless and immutable economic laws which govern the important operations of a money-using economy, Post Keynesian models consequently deal with human beings for whom the future is uncertain and not statistically predictable.

Hicks reached a similar judgement and wrote:

> I am bold enough to conclude, from these considerations that the usefulness of 'statistical' or 'stochastic' methods in economics is a good deal less than is now conventionally supposed. We have no business to turn to them automatically; we should always ask ourselves, before we apply them, whether they are appropriate to the problem at hand. Very often they are not.[14]

Human beings in Post Keynesian models understand that those who hesitate to spend today's income are saved to make a decision another day. Conversely, in a neoclassical Say's Law world, decision-makers never hesitate to commit all of today's earnings to the purchase of goods and services so that all of today's resources are fully employed.

In a Post Keynesian analysis, if decision-makers are uncertain about the future and timid in their entrepreneurial pursuits, then they protect themselves against possible erroneous spending decisions by maintaining a liquid position in terms of cash and other financial assets. The desire to maintain liquidity and therefore avoid future unpleasant surprises if unforeseen obligations arise, becomes a crucial focal point. In neoclassical models, on the other hand, there is never a long-run need for money or liquidity to protect oneself from future unforeseen and unforeseeable unfortunate circumstances – since there will be none.

This Post Keynesian emphasis on evolving economic affairs in a world with an uncertain future is diametrically opposed to the nicety and mathematical elegance of the neoclassical analysis. In a sense, the Post Keynesians seem analogous to the little boy in the fable of 'The Emperor's Clothes', who calls attention to the nakedness of the ruler. This has irritated leaders of the neoclassical school who feel that they are being unfairly attacked by a school of thought that may have some caustic criticisms but is itself devoid of any scientific theoretical framework. Neoclassical economists complain that Post Keynesians are rejecting an analysis which is fundamental to developing economics as a science – the general equilibrium system. For example, Nobel Prize winner Robert Solow of the Massachusetts Institute of Technology complains:

> Modern Post Keynesians...seem to say that Keynes's basic contribution to macro-theory was the rejection of the equilibrium concept as hopelessly ahistorical. The textbook model, in its relentless addiction to model building has 'confused historical time and logical time' and ignored the essential importance of finance. Now some of this is almost incomprehensible to me, and the part I do understand strikes me as way out of proportion. It is certainly the case that much equilibrium theory and even disequilibrium theory of the IS–LM variety is negligent in historical detail and of the irreversibilities that history builds into the economy. But I can not imagine any IS–LM-connoisseur who, confronted with that argument, would not reply: 'yes, that's fair comment'. The comparative advantage of the model-building method is certainly not in its ability to reflect the texture of historical detail....In using a model to interpret a particular historical incident, one should certainly leave plenty of room for those nuggets of context that may condition the whole episode and may even determine important aspects of the outcome. It is harder for me to see how this point can be erected into a principle of doctrine.... Thus far so-called post-Keynesianism seems to be more a state of mind than a theory![15]

In the eyes of neoclassical Keynesians, the critical comments of the Post Keynesians do not justify jettisoning the analytical model so carefully nurtured by so many neoclassical brains over the years.

In turn, Post Keynesians believe that responses such as those of Professors Solow and Tobin miss the bigger theoretical picture. In trying to protect the neoclassical trees that they laboured so hard to create, neoclassicists are apparently blind to the bigger forest in which we live. To a neoclassicist, the Post Keynesians have no theoretical structure to replace the neoclassical analysis. To a Post Keynesian, the theoretical structure of the neoclassical scholars is based on inapplicable axioms and cannot solve real-world problems, just as the theoretical Euclidean geometric system cannot solve important problems in non-Euclidean geometry.

Post Keynesians insist that Keynes began a revolution. He constructed a new theoretical approach by overthrowing some fundamental axioms that are basic to the neoclassical analysis. Although the Post Keynesian model might not be as sophisticated and polished as the neoclassical scheme, it is neither as shopworn nor misleading.

Neoclassical Keynesians believe that the Post Keynesians are unduly rigid in their defence of Keynes's analysis. As Professor Solow readily admits, in the real world, actual experience need not always and immediately reflect a full employment general equilibrium outcome. Solow writes:

> Adjustment processes are at best slow...disequilibrium can persist for a long time. Macroeconomic equilibrium is thus vulnerable to all sorts of disturbances. Here I can offer an olive branch to the post Keynesian school. One of the ways in which history and historical time matter for macroeconomics is that they can affect the adjustment process very intimately. Financial and other commitments from the past, and expectations and apprehensions about the future, can easily interfere with the economy's ability to adapt to changes in aggregate demand and supply.[16]

It would appear that there can be peace between the neoclassical Keynesians and the Post Keynesians if only the latter would accept the belief – as an article of faith – that in the short run, Keynes's criticism may have some validity in that there can be temporary departures from full employment as adjustments to changes in the economy take place. But *in the long run*, if the market is free to work things out, in good Panglossian terms, the best of all possible outcomes would evolve as the economy automatically achieves the general equilibrium outcome presumed under Say's Law.

Yet, as we have already indicated in our discussion of Professor Friedman's emphasis on long-run predictions as the fundamental criteria of 'good' economic theory, Keynes, in his 'in the long run we'll all be dead' remark had summarily and forcefully rejected this long-run strand of argument as irrelevant to the real world.

The Post Keynesians, like Keynes, reject the view that the system is self-righting in the long run. In the next chapter, we will see how this has fostered policy as well as theoretical differences between Post Keynesians and all schools of economics which are based on the neoclassical approach.

NOTES

1. M. Friedman, *Essays in Positive Economics*, University of Chicago Press, Chicago, 1953, reprinted 1966 (italics added).
2. M. Friedman, 'A Theoretical Framework For Monetary Analysis' in R. J. Gordon (ed.), *Milton Friedman's Monetary Framework: A Debate With His Critics*, Univ. of Chicago Press, Chicago, 1974, p. 27.
3. J. M. Keynes, *A Tract on Monetary Reform*, reprinted as vol. IV, of *The Collected Writings of John Maynard Keynes*, Macmillan, London, 1971, p. 65.
4. J. Tobin, 'Theoretical Issues in Macroeconomics', in G. R. Feiwel (ed.), *Issues in Contemporary Macroeconomics and Distribution*, State University of New York Press, Albany, 1985, p. 115.
5. Published in *The Collective Writings of John Maynard Keynes*, Vol XIV, Macmillan, London, 1973, p. 297.
6. J. R. Hicks, *Economic Perspectives*, Oxford University Press, Oxford, 1977, p. vii.
7. R. Lucas and T. Sargent, *Rational Expectations and Econometric Practices*, University of Minnesota Press, Minneapolis, 1981, pp. xi–xiii .
8. J. M. Keynes, *The General Theory of Employment, Interest and Money*, Harcourt Brace, New York, 1936, pp. 149–50.
9. Ibid., pp. 161–3.
10. Since earning income involves disutility, while producible goods are assumed to be the only scarce things which generate utility, then so long as it is presumed that probability structures governing future outcomes are, in the long run, 'knowable' (that is, ergodic, see *infra*), it would not be 'rational' (that is, optimizing) behaviour to engage in income earning activity merely to hold, in the long run, liquid assets rather than spend it on real goods and services.
11. J. R. Hicks, *Causality in Economics*, Basic Books, New York, 1979, pp. 37–8.
12. P. Davidson, *Money and the Real World* (rev. edn), Macmillan, London, 1978, p. 373.
13. Ibid., p. 373.
14. J. R. Hicks, *Causality in Economics*, op. cit., p. 129.
15. R. M. Solow, 'Alternative Approaches to Macroeconomics', *Canadian Journal of Economics*, 1976, pp. 343–4.
16. Ibid., p. 345.

5. Uncertainty and Money

Time is a device which prevents everything from happening at once. The production of commodities takes time; and the consumption of capital goods and consumer durables takes considerable time. Hence, decision-makers recognize that the outcomes in terms of profit and/or utility to be obtained from most economic activities require a significant amount of historical time to pass between the moment a decision is made and the time the consequences are experienced. Each of us, when we face an economic decision whose costs and benefits are embedded in future events, has to decide whether the economic environment concerning this prospective action can be characterized as falling into one of the following environments:

1. *An objectivity probability environment.* In this situation, the decision-maker believes that the past is a statistically reliable guide to the future and that an analysis of past relative frequencies of outcomes therefore provides a statistically reliable probability analysis of future prospects. This case involves what neoclassical economists call the rational expectations hypothesis (REH) where knowledge regarding future consequences of today's decisions involve a confluence of subjective expected probabilities and objective (given by immutable laws) probabilities.

2. *A subjective probability environment.* At the moment of choice, the decision-maker believes that he or she can order or array all possible future outcomes that he or she can conceive of in terms of subjective probabilities.[1] In this situation, there is no necessary requirement that the short-run subjective probabilities must coincide with these objective distributions.[2] In the individual's mind, only his subjective probabilities regarding

46

future prospects at the moment governs the choice made. In a true Social Darwinian style, however, neoclassical economists proclaim that those decision-makers who succeed will act 'as if' their subjective probabilities correctly reflected the objective probabilities that are presumed to prevail.

3. *The uncertainty environment.* The decision-maker believes that during the lapse of calendar time between the moment of choice and the date(s) of pay-off, unforeseeable changes will occur. In other words, the decision-maker believes that *no* information regarding future prospects exists today and therefore the future is not calculable, even if she is competent to perform the mathematical operations necessary to calculate probabilities of conditional events, providing she had the necessary information. This is uncertainty (or ignorance about future consequences) in the sense of Keynes and the Post Keynesians,[3] and the longer the lapse between choice and consequence, all other things being equal, the more likely the individual is to suspect she is making a decision in an uncertain environment.

For Keynes and the Post Keynesians, probabilities involve calculable risks (knowledge), while uncertainty is ignorance about forthcoming prospects. In neoclassical theory there is no concept equivalent to Keynes's uncertainty – that is, ignorance of the future. Using Friedman's positivistic methodology, ignorance is banished from the analysis by presuming that decision-makers acted 'as if' they have knowledge – risky though it may be – about the future.

Keynes and the Post Keynesians attempt to provide a more *general* theory where some basically routine activities may be associated with probabilistic risk, but others involve decisions which recognize one's ignorance of the future. In the real world, individuals continually face the difficulty of reaching a judgement about whether past experience provides any guidelines regarding future outcomes. Should one blithely presume the uniformity and consistency of economic processes so that future events can be discerned from what appears to be historical patterns? Can one completely specify all possible outcomes of any choice and then order one's preferences regarding all possible prospects? Is there no fear of tragedy if one incorrectly assumes uniformity imposed by immutable economic laws, at least during the calendar time between choice and outcome? Or does the agent believe he or she is ignorant regarding the future? Uncertainty or ignorance regarding the future is in the eye of the beholder. No ubiquitous rule can be specified in advance regarding how any individual makes such a judgement as to which of the objective, subjective or uncertainty environments described above she is operating in – although Keynes argued that the longer the lapse between action and consequence, the more likely the beholder is to fear the unknown.

The belief that all economic decisions are, *and should be*, 'as if' a reliably forecastable future underlies every aspect of neoclassical analysis. So long as the future accurately reflects historical patterns, then decision-makers are deemed to make persistently 'correct' rational forecasts. Hence if all market actions are based on rational expectations, then the result must maximize the welfare of society and lead to full employment and stable prices. This is basic to the logical foundation upon which the *laissez-faire* philosophy is based.

More sophisticated neoclassical models recognize that the gathering and statistical analysis of historical databases are costly. Moreover, every individual may not be equally skilled or sufficiently motivated enough to afford to gather, and correctly interpret, past information in order to tease out statistically reliable guides for the future from the historical market data. In some models, the necessary mental ability (and/or the income to afford the necessary resources) to discern statistical patterns may be beyond some (or all?) the inhabitants of an economy. Nevertheless, an overriding neoclassical presumption is that an omnipotent 'Mother Nature' 'knows' the underlying immutable economic structure. (If the structure changes over time, then these changes are predetermined and hence are also known to Mother Nature).[4]

The problem regarding the individual's ignorance of the governing probabilities in these sophisticated models is reduced to a problem of comparing the short-run cost of obtaining and processing sufficient information (that is, forcing Mother Nature to release her economic secrets)[5] vis-à-vis the benefits to be derived from making error-free forecasts. In the long run, those who invest enough resources into correctly forecasting the future on the basis of some presumed probability environment will survive and thrive for, by definition, they will not make persistent errors.

Finally, in recent years, some perceptive neoclassical theorists have recognized that, in reality, some people do continually exhibit ignorance regarding the future. In order to make the problem tractable to neoclassical techniques, however, this ignorance is finessed in one of two ways. The first appeals to the concept of 'Bayesian priors' to introduce probabilistic concepts into the analysis. The second way introduces a *short-run option to wait* while 'learning' about the future; in the long run, however, it is presumed that enough learning has occurred so that a choice based on probabilistic circumstances can be made.

THE BAYESIAN APPROACH

Some neoclassical models argue that all optimizing, self-interested economic decision-makers will employ something statisticians call 'Bayesian priors' based on the 'principle of indifference', to evaluate future consequences whenever they do not currently possess *any* information about the governing probabilities. Whenever there is a total lack of past statistical evidence regarding the probabilities of alternative future outcomes, then the Bayesian approach states that one should initially assign 'equal probabilities' to each alternative as one's subjective probability (or Bayesian prior) estimate. As time passes and evidence is gathered, one then adjusts the initial equally probable 'priors' towards the relative frequencies observed via the empirical evidence that has been gathered.

So long as it is presumed that the evidence is being generated by a timeless set of probabilities, then this Bayesian approach to the formation of probabilistic expectations is efficient (that is, technically rational in a neoclassical sense) as a Darwinian 'learning by doing' process which permits the survivors to make choices 'as if' they know the 'true' governing objective probabilities. In the long run, then, as immutable probabilities governing future outcomes are presumed to exist and persist, the concept of ignorance is an empty set, since surviving agents behave as if they have perfect probabilistic foreknowledge about the future. In his *General Theory,* Keynes specifically denied the usefulness of the Bayesian priors approach when he discussed investment decisions under uncertainty:

> Nor can we rationalise our behaviour by arguing that to a man in a state of ignorance errors in either direction are equally probable, so that there remains a mean actuarial expectation based on equiprobabilities. For it can easily be shown that the assumption of arithmetically equal probabilities based on a state of ignorance leads to absurdities.[6]

THE OPTION TO WAIT APPROACH

The neoclassical alternative to Bayesian priors is a short-run 'option to wait' approach, which presumes that, in the long run, information will always be available; hence waiting is not a long-run choice. For example, in one variant developed by Kreps, the analysis of 'waiting' presumes that, at the initial instant, the individual does not possess the information required to make a rational decision. Accordingly, the individual postpones the decision until at some early future date the agent receives information about which state prevails[7] at a later future pay-off date. Thus, it is presumed that the agent 'will learn the true state'[8] at some time in the future before the agent is required to complete all his or her choices. Waiting, therefore, is presumed to be only a short-run phenomenon persisting only until information is received; in the long run waiting behaviour is not optimal in the neoclassical analysis – *unless the information is never received*! But the option to wait is always associated with a 'preference for flexibility' *until* sufficient information is obtained. There is, therefore, an implicit assumption that information exists and that one is only waiting for a Turing machine to complete and make available its calculations on information regarding tastes, trends and so on for the day after tomorrow.

If, however, one does not presume the pre-existence of information, how can one 'know' that agents will receive 'information about which state prevails' at some time before they are all dead? Keynes insisted that decisions not to buy products (to save) did

> ...*not* necessitate a decision to have dinner or to buy a pair of boots a week hence or a year hence or to consume any specified thing at any specified date....It is not a substitution of future consumption demand for current consumption demand – it is a net diminution of such demand.[9]

In other words, Keynes's argument is that there need not be any intertemporal substitution of real expenditures tomorrow for those postponed today while waiting for information. In the long run, people may still feel ignorant regarding the future and hence want to stay liquid. Hence in Keynes's 'General Theory' *there can exist a long-period unemployment equilibrium* and Say's Law need not be applicable.

There is empirical evidence to support Keynes's belief that, over their lifetimes, human beings do avoid spending all their income, preferring instead to remain liquid and to wait. For example, when researchers at the University of Wisconsin analysed data on consumption and incomes of elderly individuals, their statistical analysis showed that:

> ...the elderly do not dissave to finance their consumption at retirement... [the elderly] spend less on consumption goods and services (save significantly more) than the nonelderly at all levels of income. Moreover, the oldest of the elderly save the most at given levels of income.[10]

Thus the facts suggest that life becomes more uncertain as one ages (in Keynes's sense) leading the elderly to 'wait' without making a decision to spend their earned claims on resources. Such behaviour is neither rational according to neoclassical theory, nor compatible with Kreps's short-run option to wait – unless one is willing to admit that, even in the long run, 'information about which state will prevail' may not exist!

Despite this evidence, and more than a half-century after Keynes wrote, sophisticated neoclassical analysis will only admit the possibility of short-run 'Keynesian' outcomes, and still argues in favour of the familiar long-run homilies embedded in the neutral money axiom. *Laissez-faire* is still held to be the best of all possible worlds in the long run.

A cursory view may therefore suggest to some that there are some strands of neoclassical short-run thought which appear to be logically compatible with Keynes's analysis of 'waiting' human behaviour under conditions of uncertainty. Nevertheless, the other behavioural aspect, the 'damn the torpedoes' 'animal spirit' of Keynes's entrepreneur is still missing from all neoclassical models.

In sum, despite the millions of man-hours allocated to polishing and developing the neoclassical model, proponents of this approach have still failed to recognize that Keynes's analysis is the more general case. Instead, neoclassical analysts treat Keynes's theory as a *special* case, a short-run anomaly to neoclassical theory where *already existing information* is not readily and freely available to decision-makers. Such an analytical approach suggests that the difficulty of collecting and analysing information permits individuals to make errors in the short run. Hence the economy may not immediately achieve a position of long-run economic bliss.

Another model which permits short-run defects in a neoclassical world involves 'asymmetric information'. Such models presume that some decision-makers can better analyse the existing and extensive database than others. This asymmetric information approach permits some neoclassical economists to acknowledge that Keynes's analysis may have some relevance in determining short-run, or what neoclassicists call 'temporary equilibrium'. Nevertheless, in the long run, neoclassical logic still argues that Keynes's method degenerates into a long-run empty box. What neoclassical scholars always knew was the absolute truth regarding the efficiency of individual choice in free markets to provide maximum welfare and full employment without inflation remains unfazed. The philosophy of *laissez-faire*, therefore, remains untarnished in the long run, while Keynes is viewed via neoclassical blinkers.

NOTES

1. J. Von Neumann and O. Morgenstern, *Theory of Games and Economic Behavior* (3rd edn), Princeton University Press, Princeton, 1953, believe that the subjective probabilities are in terms of relative frequencies, while L. Savage, *The Foundation of Statistics,* John Wiley, New York, 1954, defines subjective probabilities in terms of degrees of conviction.
2. If the subjective and objective probabilities tended to be the same, then the decision-maker would believe that he or she is operating in the objective probability environment explained above.
3. Keynes conceived of a 'life without probabilities' as conceptually quite different from neoclassical views. He indicated that, by uncertainty, he did '...not mean merely to distinguish what is known for certain from what is only probable. The game of roulette is not subject, in this sense to uncertainty....The sense in which I am using the terms is that ... there is no scientific basis on which to form any calculable probability whatever. We simply do not know' (J. M. Keynes, 'The General Theory', *Quarterly Journal of Economics*, 1937, reprinted in *The Collected Writings of John Maynard Keynes,* vol. XIV, Macmillan, London, 1971, p. 113). Moreover, Keynes added, 'the hypothesis of a calculable future leads to a wrong interpretation of the principles of behaviour' [Ibid, p. 122].
    For Keynes, the 'long period employment' need never be equal to the long-run equilibrium level of full employment predicted by Say's Law. He attributed this difference in employment outcomes to agents demanding money, not to spend, but for liquidity to protect themselves from an uncertain and unpredictable future, and to entrepreneurs' investment decisions based on 'vague and more various possibilities which make up his state of expectations' (J. M. Keynes, *The General Theory of Employment, Interest and Money,* Harcourt Brace, New York, 1936, p. 24n).
4. Keynes noted that the difference between a dynamic system and a static economy involved 'not the economy under observation which is moving in one case and stationary in the other, but our expectations of the future environment which are shifting in one case and stationary in the other' [J. M. Keynes, *The Collected Writings of John Maynard Keynes,* Vol. XIV, Macmillan, London, 1973, p. 511. Keynes argued in his *General Theory* [p. 294] that we 'cannot even begin to discuss the effect of changing expectations on current activities except in monetary terms'. But changing expectations can occur only if future probability structures are *unknown*

currently because *no information can exist* today regarding future outcomes.

5. These costs may be very high, but since the data determining the future is already programmed into the operation of the structure, it is potentially available to those individuals who could and would expend enough time, energy and mental activity to build a Turing machine to discover it.

6. J. M. Keynes, *The General Theory of Employment, Interest and Money*, op. cit., p. 152.

7. D. M. Kreps, *Notes On A Theory of Choice*, Westview Press, Boulder, Col., 1988, p. 142.

8. Ibid., p. 187.

9. J. M. Keynes, *The General Theory of Employment, Interest and Money*, op. cit., p. 210.

10. S. Danziger, J. van der Haag, E. Smolensky and M. Taussig, 'The Life Cycle Hypothesis and the Consumption Behavior of the Elderly', *Journal of Post Keynesian Economics*, **5**, Winter 1982–83, p. 210.

6.   The Role of Contracts and Money in Theory and the Real World

Keynes and the Post Keynesians base their economic analysis on the following inductive propositions:

1. Modern monetary economies do not possess any automatic mechanism that assures a tendency towards full employment of resources over time.
2. Underemployment equilibrium is a recurring phenomenon in economies that use money contracts and money payments to organize production and exchange activities.
3. Therefore, the existence of underemployment equilibrium must be associated with the characteristics of money and the use of contracts to organize production.

All living organisms have to solve the basic economic problems of what to produce, how to produce it, and how the fruits of production are distributed amongst the members of any group. Most lower life forms solve these problems as members of an organizational and societal structure (for example, beaver and ant colonies, schools of fish, herds of elephants, and so on). Although the survival of these lower life forms depends on their ability to solve these basic economic problems, none of these life forms *interacts* via contracts, money and markets to achieve the objectives of the species in question. Only in recent times, and only in developed societies, has mankind created and utilized the institutions of money, markets and contracts as the primary tools in resolving the economic production and distribution problems of the community.

The standard of living of any human communities that fail to develop these institutions of money and markets, including some human communities isolated from the economic development of the last 500 years, are still closely tied, via Malthusian principles, to their natural environment. When nature is bountiful, these communities thrive; when the environment turns bleak, the population declines. For centuries, from Biblical times until the end of feudalism, almost all societies were similarly tied to the natural environment. But, beginning with the Renaissance and the development of money, financial institutions, contracts and markets as we know them, human beings gained the ability to sever the Malthusian link between the size of the population and the generosity or frugality of nature. As markets and the use of money developed in a community, the residents gained the means to thrive with ever rising standards of living, even during periods of harsh natural conditions.

Conversely, only man, of all life forms, seems to suffer from the inability to maintain the full employment of available resources in the production processes necessary to ensure the survival of the species and its standard of living. For Post Keynesians, the existence of markets, finance and monetary institutions is important in the explanation of the economic evolution of *Homo sapiens* and their superior economic level relative to other life forms. But this superiority is a double-edged sword; it permits rising standards of living, but, under certain *man-made* conditions, it can subjugate a large proportion of the population to poverty and even starvation at the same time that society possesses idle resources which could alleviate this poverty, if only they were fully and voluntarily employed .

This then is the Keynes–Post Keynesian paradox resulting from the human use of money and markets. When wisely directed, a market–monetary system can provide living conditions well above subsistence levels as scarce resources are fully and cleverly employed. On the other hand, when left to the vagueness of a *laissez-faire* environment, market systems have shown a propensity, at times, to break down and fail to provide the prosperous standards of living that the system is capable of delivering. Resources that would be scarce if the economy was operating efficiently are allowed to lie idle.

Post Keynesians associate the human institutions of money and the financial, contractual and market system as essential features which yield both these great advantages and outstanding flaws of the economic society in which modern man lives. Especially relevant to the cause of these blessings and deficiencies is the time-orientation of markets and contracts, especially the money-wage contract used to organize production processes, and the need of businessmen and households to maintain liquidity to meet all forthcoming contractual obligations.

Liquidity involves the ability to meet all monetary contractual obligations when they become due. By definition, only money possesses the property of being the medium of contractual settlement. Hence, the holding of money involves the possession of *the* asset of ultimate liquidity. Other assets – for example, traded corporate securities, government bonds and treasury bills, money market mutual funds, and so on – may possess various degrees of liquidity, dependent on the existence and extent of a resaleable market for that particular asset, the resale market's degree of organization, continuity and orderliness. These market attributes determine how quickly and conveniently, and at what cost, the traded asset can be converted into money to meet a liquidity need. Many real assets, such as second-hand furniture and other consumer durables, although having some – and often significant value in use for their possessors – are illiquid in that no organized and orderly market exists for their resaleability to obtain cash.

Money is first and foremost a human institution, making liquidity a peculiarly human problem only associated with developed market economies. In the world we live in, money is not shells or beads, or peanuts, or bananas or any other commodity easily produced by labour in the private sector. It is inextricably tied to society's laws governing the banking system and to the use of money contracts to purchase goods and to hire labour on a time–use basis for productive purposes. In fact, with the legal abolition of slavery, the dominant method for employing human labour in modern economies involves the use of the money-wage contract.

The almost universal use of these raw material purchase and labour hire contracts by business managers to organize the inputs in the production process is what creates the major demand for liquidity by entrepreneurs to meet their cash outflow commitments resulting from these 'forward' contracts.

THE TIME ORIENTATION OF CONTRACTS

There are two types of time-oriented contracts in real-world developed economies – spot contracts and forward contracts. A spot contract is a legal agreement between parties where the seller agrees to make an immediate delivery of something and the buyer agrees to make an immediate payment of money. A forward contract is a legal obligation between the contracting parties that specifies a future date (or dates) for both delivery and money payment. Since production takes time, the hiring of labour and the purchase of materials to be used in any productive activity must precede the date when the finished product will be available to the entrepreneur for delivery to buyers. For any lengthy production process, hiring and raw material purchase transactions will require forward contracting to permit entrepreneurial control of the production operation and the efficient sequencing of labour, capital and raw material inputs in producing the final product for sale.

Post Keynesians argue that business managers know that, in a world of uncertainty, 'to err is human' and therefore entrepreneurs realize that their expectations of sales and profits may be wrong in both the short and long run. Were human nature not tempted to take a chance, to possess the 'animal spirits' that urges action rather than inaction, to 'damn the torpedoes and move full speed ahead', then entrepreneurial activities would quickly wither away. The courage of the entrepreneur is an essential characteristic of successful and prosperous economies. As Davidson and Davidson proclaim, 'Society admires this courage; that is why we admire the entrepreneur more than we admire the actuary'.[1]

Only a fool, however, would rush in to challenge the unknown future without some strategy to protect against failure. Smart and successful entrepreneurs are no fools. They only undertake challenges when they can enter into long-duration forward contracts with workers and suppliers, where the date(s) and deliveries and money payments – and hence liabilities – are fixed in advance. So long as entrepreneurs feel that they have sufficient liquidity to meet these forward contractual obligations, they can adopt the 'damn the torpedoes' philosophy safe in the knowledge that their entrepreneurship cannot sink before the final output has been produced and is available for sale.

Modern society has developed the institution of legally enforceable forward money contracts to permit the contracting parties to possess a measure of control over future performance and cash flows, even in the face of ignorance regarding future real economic conditions. Money contracts are the only agreements among the parties which are enforceable under the civil law. Time is of the essence of any contract under the civil law. Each party to a contract believes, at the signing of the contract, that carrying out the contractual terms will enhance his/her own well-being. (This mutual beneficial agreement is known as 'the contract curve solution' in economics or a meeting of the minds in law.) If, as neoclassical economics assumes, the future was calculable, then there should be no need to require legal enforcement of forward contracts since it is in the best interests of both parties to carry out the agreed upon terms of the contract.

Yet, so long as the future is uncertain (in the sense of Keynes), each party also 'knows' that when tomorrow becomes today, one or the other party may be unable and/or unwilling to carry out the terms of the contract.[2] Each contracting party is also aware that if the other fails to perform as required in the contract, the state will enforce, in lieu of performance, a monetary payment for any damages to be made to the aggrieved party. Provided that the law of contracts is enforced by all civilized societies, contracting parties are thereby provided legal assurances regarding cash flows even if an unpredictable event occurs.

Accordingly, the organization of production and exchange transaction on a contractual basis permits the seller and the buyer to exert some control over cash flows in an otherwise unpredictable future. For example, contracts assure entrepreneurs' future performance from workers and suppliers, or at least the ability to avoid pecuniary damages, in return for a fixed monetary payment. Consequently, no matter how bad today's decision to purchase inputs for the production process proves from hindsight, the business manager has limited his maximum liability to his monetary contractual commitment. If each contracting party possesses enough liquidity to meet these future cash commitments, then each 'knows' that he or she can economically survive any future disaster involving this transaction.

On the other hand, in order logically and rigorously to demonstrate the benefits of a *laissez-faire* system, neoclassical analysis requires that all *contractual payments be made at the initial instant of time*.[3] In other words, the logical conclusions that a free market economy will automatically achieve a full employment, inflation-free equilibrium not only requires a calculable future but also has as a logical prerequisite that all payments for goods and services must be made at the initial instant of time – even if delivery is not expected until tomorrow, next year, or even next century. For example, Berkeley Professor Roy Radner has characterized the circumstances involved in the fundamental contractual situation required for neoclassical theory as follows:

> An elementary contract in this market will consist of the purchase (or sale) of some specified number of units of a specified commodity to be delivered at a specified location and date, if and only if a specified elementary event occurs. Payment for this purchase is to be made now (at the beginning).[4]

Professor Radner's summary of the neoclassical view of contracts and payments is: 'In the above interpretation of the economy, all accounts are settled before the history of the economy begins.'[5]

If all accounts are settled 'before the history of the economy begins', then, obviously, neither managers nor households, nor buyers, nor sellers need worry about liquidity. By assumption, there are no contractual obligations outstanding that will become due at any future date! Accordingly, neoclassical economists deal with the problem of liquidity as they have dealt with all the issues raised by Keynes in differentiating his 'General Theory' from the neoclassical analysis: they define away the problem.

Yet liquidity is a problem that each one of us has to deal with almost every day of our lives – and certainly every time we try to balance our cheque book. The problem of trying to maintain a liquid position is almost a universal difficulty which colours almost every major economic decision we make in the real world that we inhabit. Nevertheless, it is banished from the process of decision-making in neoclassical analysis.

The neoclassical presumption that all payments in an economy occur at the beginning of time is one of those 'host of conditions of dubious realism' that Professor Tobin mentioned as necessary to formulate 'rigorously' and prove the beneficence of the 'invisible hand' of free markets. Without these conditions, neoclassical theorists can never rigorously prove that free markets assure full employment and the optimum allocation of resources. Hence without this unrealistic proviso, the powerful neoclassical outcomes which justify *laissez-faire* policies are logically insupportable!

Post Keynesians argue that this necessary neoclassical requirement that all payments be made at the initial instant emasculates the need for any concept of liquidity. It prevents neoclassical theory from making any connection with reality. For, in the real world, liquidity is the name of the economic game. Hence, Post Keynesians argue, neoclassical economists are throwing away the baby with the bathwater when they assume away, as they must, any of the problems of liquidity that plague people who are engaged in real-world market transactions.

THE NEOCLASSICAL VS POST KEYNESIAN VIEW OF MONEY AND CONTRACTS

If this Post Keynesian argument is correct, then, one might inquire how can neoclassical economists remain loyal to the neoclassical model which is so firmly rooted in unrealistic conditions regarding payments?

Some neoclassical theorists exercise damage control by putting the best possible spin on Professor Tobin's 'bad news' problem. These economists claim that the sophisticated neoclassical general equilibrium model serves a useful function in demonstrating why a free market system can *never* reach an optimum allocation in the real world. For example, Cambridge Professor Frank Hahn has argued that neoclassical systems are

> ...very useful for instance when one comes to argue with someone who maintains that we need not worry about exhaustible resources because they will always have prices which ensure their 'proper' use. Of course there are many things wrong with this contention but a quick way of disposing of the claim is to note that an equilibrium must be an assumption he is making for the economy and then to show why the economy can not be in this state.[6]

Hahn states that the argument as to why the economy cannot be in 'this state' revolves on the problems of payments and

> ...on the inadequate treatment of time and uncertainty by the construction. This negative role of equilibrium models I consider sufficient justification for it, for practical men and ill-trained theorists everywhere in the world do not understand what they are claiming to be the case when they claim a beneficent and coherent role for the invisible hand. But for descriptive purposes of course this negative role is hardly a recommendation.[7]

Other scholars, enamoured by what Tobin calls the 'elegant, rigorous, mathematical powerful' neoclassical analysis, which gives economics the appearance of a hard-science theoretical core, defend the neoclassical system for as they see it, according to Professor Tobin:

> It is the only game in town. It especially enchants those who were drawn into the profession more because it challenges their mathematical and logical skills than because it might help to solve real world puzzles and problems. They are largely disposed to regard general equilibrium propositions as reference points, and to assign burdens of proof to anyone who consciously or unconsciously alleges otherwise. Supporting this attitude is the methodology of positive economics. The patent and admitted unrealism of assumptions does not matter.[8]

The last refuge of the neoclassical ideologue is the methodology of Friedman's positive economics where 'The relevant question to ask about the 'assumptions' of a theory is not whether they are descriptively realistic, for they never are, but whether they are a sufficiently good approximation for the purpose at hand'.[9]

This positive economics methodological approach thereby subtly avoids having to deal with the entire question of realism. It finesses the question of whether the theoretical model provides a reasonable match with the essential conditions in the real world. Instead, the question becomes, according to Professor Tobin, 'whether the outcomes of the system as a whole are *as if* they were the solutions of the postulated system'.[10]

In sum, defenders of neoclassical economics have adopted a variety of strategies which more or less insulate them from admitting the inapplicability of their models to real-world problems. They can always claim that assumptions such as the neutrality of money are, in Professor Friedman's words, 'sufficiently good approximations' even if they are patently false.

For example, Professor Robert Lucas of the University of Chicago has elaborated on this point. In attempting to explain why the unrealistic neoclassical model dominates the majority of the economics profession's way of analysing economic problems, Lucas states:

> ... it must be because people perceive useful analogies between the patently artificial world of the model and the world we live in, and not because they are unable to distinguish between the two worlds. If so, then successful criticism must go beyond an enumeration of the ways in which the model and reality differ to offer some perception of the nature of the analogies that are being drawn and some argument to the effect that these analogies are misleading.[11]

This argument cleverly shifts the onus onto the critics who must persuade neoclassical economists of the delusive nature of their system. But no objective criterion is provided to measure how misleading the neoclassical analogy must be shown to be *in the long run* in order to be successful in convincing neoclassical economists of the error of their ways. Moreover, given the heavy investment that most professional economists make in learning the rigorous neoclassical general equilibrium analysis in order to qualify for their PhD degrees, it should be no surprise that the Post Keynesian arguments which appeal to the need for realism have failed to convince many neoclassicists of their analogies' misleading ways.

Unlike neoclassical scholars, Post Keynesians put a strong emphasis on the importance of basing theory upon realistic assumptions – especially regarding the role of money in the economy. The Post Keynesian model of the economic system may not have the same rigorous mathematical beauty of the neoclassical model, but it is a better description of reality. Whereas neoclassical scholars have invested an untold number of man-hours in the last half-century in refining their unrealistic model, Post Keynesians, being much smaller in number, have been able to muster only a small fraction of those man-hours to develop their model of a decentralized market economy moving irresistibly through historic time into the uncertain future. Nevertheless the constant criticisms of the latter have made some impact in forcing a few neoclassical scholars to reevaluate their approach.

We have seen that a fundamental logical difference between neoclassical logic and the Keynes–Post Keynesian approach revolves around how the concepts of money and contractual payments are dealt with in the two models. As some neoclassical economists have grown more aware of the lack of realism in their approach to the problems of contractual payments, they have tried to examine how critical these dubious conditions are for the outcome of their theoretical analysis and whether they can get the same results without these drastic assumptions. Neoclassical Nobel Prize winner Kenneth Arrow of Stanford University collaborated with Professor Frank Hahn of Cambridge University to analyse scrupulously the analytical basis for neoclassical analysis and compare it with the real world. Their study showed that:

> The terms in which contracts are made matter. In particular, if money is the good in terms of which contracts are made, then the prices of goods in terms of money are of special significance. This is not the

case if we consider an economy without a past and without a future. Keynes wrote that 'the importance of money essentially flows from it being a link between the present and the future' to which we add that it is important also because it is a link between the past and the present. *If a serious monetary theory comes to be written. the fact that contracts are indeed made in terms of money will be of considerable importance.*[12]

With this statement, Arrow and Hahn have indicated that, despite all the writings and rhetoric of neoclassical economic scholars, they have yet to write 'a serious monetary theory'. Yet the Post Keynesians, following the lead of Keynes, would argue that they themselves have developed a 'serious monetary theory' which gives primary attention to the economic role of money contracts in general and the money-wage contract in particular.

The existence of fixed money contracts for forward delivery and payment is fundamental to the concepts of liquidity and money in Post Keynesian theory. If, in the aggregate, businessmen expect that it would be profitable to increase production, then they will be required to sign additional raw material purchase and labour hire contracts. This increase in contractual commitments requires managers to obtain additional liquidity in order to meet these additional production commitments as they become due. The ability of the banking system to create money (bank deposits for entrepreneurs) to provide business managers with the necessary finance to pay for these *increases* in production flows is, therefore, an essential expansionary element in the operation of any non-neutral monetary production economy.

If entrepreneurs cannot obtain additional bank money commitments when, in the aggregate, they wish to increase hiring and production flows, then businessmen will not be able to meet additional payroll and material purchase obligations. Accordingly, in the absence of the creation of additional bank money deposits,[13] managers will not be willing to sign additional hiring contracts, and long-run employment growth will be stymied, even when future demand is expected to be sufficiently profitable to warrant expansion. In this situation money is not neutral – a shortage of money can hold up the expansion of real output! Under such circumstances, it is obvious that the Central Bank, by controlling the ability of commercial banks to make loans to businessmen, can affect the economy's real output and employment rate – even in the long run.

If, on the other hand, entrepreneurs can obtain sufficient liquidity via additional bank loan commitments from their bankers to finance expansion in their working capital, then firms can proceed with their increased production plans. The managers' only (and not insignificant) worry then will be whether expectations of profitability from the sales of additional output at a future gestation date will come true. If, when the future becomes the present, these profit expectations prove to be justified, then managers will have sufficient sales revenue on hand to pay off their working capital bank loans. When managers use their sales revenue to repay existing loans, this provides evidence to their bankers of the entrepreneurs' creditworthiness. Hence bankers will be willing to make new loans to managers to begin a new production cycle.

To ensure full employment growth in an entrepreneurial economic system, managers of business firms must expect future demand to be sufficiently profitable to encourage them to borrow whatever funds are necessary to finance the level of contractual demands to ensure full employment of resources. The ready availability of increases in bank credit alone is, in this Keynes–Post Keynesian view, a necessary, but not a sufficient, condition for the economic growth of modern economies. As Keynes noted:

> ... credit is the pavement along which production travels; and the bankers if they knew their duty, would provide the transport facilities to just the extent that is required in order that the productive powers of the community can be employed at their full capacity.[14]

MONEY NEVER GROWS ON TREES

Because of the inherent uncertainties in a monetary free market economy where hiring and production depends on the decisions of a multitude of independent business managers, if entrepreneurs become fearful of the future they tend to curtail their contractual commitments to hire workers and produce output. Moreover, income earners may not spend all that they earned on the products of industry whenever they wish to increase their protection against what they 'know' is an unpredictable future.

People 'know' that it is always possible to find oneself without a job or income or sales in an economic environment which can turn hostile without warning. If people become more fearful of these possibilities, this increased anxiety can induce a reduction of purchases out of current income. The resulting increase in planned savings is used to buy protection against the unknown by increasing people's demand for money and other liquid assets. This reallocation of income from the purchase of producible goods towards liquid assets will invalidate Say's Law, unless there is an exact offsetting group of people who wish to spend a sum in excess of their earned income on the current products of industry. If, however, in the aggregate people are increasing their demand for liquidity at the expense of the demand for producible goods then there must obviously be a reduction in the market demand for the products of industry.

When this occurs in a *laissez-faire* system, entrepreneurs will experience a resulting decline in sales. This drying up of sales revenues signals managers that they are in danger of incurring further large pecuniary losses if they continue to produce at current levels. Hence, self-interest dictates that managers respond to any aggregate fall-off in demand by firing workers, reducing purchases from suppliers, and rushing to build up their own liquidity so that they can ride out the anticipated hard times. The result will be unemployed resources, recession and economic misery for as long as entrepreneurs choose to cut production in order to build up liquidity.

Keynes claimed that the characteristic that we call liquidity is only associated with durables that are neither readily produced by labour in the private sector nor easily substitutable, *for liquidity purposes*, with goods produced by labour.[15] In other words, since they are not producible by the use of labour in the private sector, money (and other liquid securities such as government bonds and listed corporate securities) does (do) not grow on trees. Hence when people reduce their spending out of income on, say, consumer goods to hold more liquidity, workers who become involuntarily unemployed in the consumer goods industries will not be rehired by the private sector to harvest additional liquid assets from money trees to meet the increased demands of people. The total effective demand for workers in the community will decline.

NEOCLASSICAL VS KEYNES'S VIEW OF THE ENTREPRENEUR AND LIQUIDITY

Nowhere is the positions of neoclassical economists and Post Keynesians more obviously diametrically opposed than in the way the phenomena of liquidity and entrepreneurship is dealt with in the two approaches. Liquidity is never a problem in a logically consistent neoclassical world, so long as either all contractual payments are presumed to be made at the initial instant and/or one possesses statistically reliable knowledge about the future.[16] In the real world, liquidity – the possession of money or other easily resaleable assets to obtain money quickly and conveniently – is the ultimate refuge for protecting one's economic self from the vagaries of the economic future. Armed with whatever one perceives as the necessary liquidity to carry through, one can embark on any adventure.

Entrepreneurs in a neoclassical world do not face the imponderables of Keynes's managers. For Keynes:

> Businessmen play a mixed game of skill and chance, the average result of which to the players are not known to those who take a hand. If human nature felt no temptation to take a chance, no satisfaction (profit apart) in constructing a factory, a railway, a mine or a farm, there might not be much investment merely as the result of cold calculation...our decisions to do something positive, the full consequences of which will be drawn out over many days to come, can only be taken as a result of animal spirits – of a spontaneous urge to action rather than inaction, and not as the outcome of a weighted average of quantitative benefits multiplied by quantitative probabilities.[17]

This Keynes–Post Keynesian view of the actions of business managers in the face of incalculable uncertainties is antithetical to the stereotypical cool, rational, calculating manager of neoclassical theory. In the Keynes and Post Keynesian concept, managers are human and fallible. In the neoclassical world where entrepreneurs have rational expectations, Professors Robert Lucas and Thomas Sargent conceive of entrepreneurs as 'robot decision-makers'. Neoclassicists see business managers as mere Turing calculating machines who do not make errors and are unswayed by human emotions, hopes, fears and foibles – veritable Mr Spocks of the free market enterprise!

Neoclassicists emphasize the logical, reckoning side of human nature, presuming that the calculated actions of individuals will inevitably create positive economic results. Fallible, error-prone managers will sustain heavy business losses until they are driven out of the market place leaving only calculating Mr Spock-type robots who consistently and correctly forecast future events. Survival, in a neoclassical analysis, requires the rational calculations of a Turing machine, not the 'animal spirits' of human beings.

Neoclassical theorists, with their emphasis on individual action and responsibility in a world with a calculable future, claim that if businessmen are unhampered by government interference, *all* economic problems will be effectively, and profitably, solved in free markets as rational economic decision-makers, on average, make long-run error-free projections.

But, again, we come back to the key question – namely that even if you accept the neoclassical analysis, how long do we individuals have to wait for this long-run state of bliss to arrive here on Earth? How long will it take until all our problems are effectively solved by independent, calculating Turing machine decision-makers? Of course, it depends on how soon those fallible and foolish human managers are weeded out by the efficient and inhuman forces of the 'invisible hand' of the marketplace. Some conservative neoclassical economists, such as Professor Robert Lucas of the University of Chicago, think that free markets can work out profitable solutions to all the economic problems very rapidly. Others, as we have already indicated, such as Nobel Prize winners Professor Robert

Solow of MIT and Professor Milton Friedman each believe that the market processes of adjustment are slower and that only in the long run (maybe years or even decades) will the market succeed.

Driven by the inexorable logic of the neoclassical analysis, however, if one accepts the axioms on which this logic is based, then all government actions in the economic sphere must, in the long run, be an obstructive force that inhabits individual action and further slows 'natural' adjustment processes. Hence, if one is consistent with the logic of neoclassical axioms and conclusions, one must believe that all government activity involving discretionary fiscal, monetary or regulatory policy inevitably reduces economic efficiency.

Keynes and the Post Keynesians, on the other hand, believe that in response to certain economic problems such as unemployment and inflation, there is a potential for disaster if the unfettered decisions and actions of individuals in a free market are permitted without any intelligent control by government. When people try to manage their affairs in light of fears of unemployment or inflation in a true *laissez-faire* environment, they may end up with a deteriorating market economy in both the short and long runs. Accordingly, the Keynes–Post Keynesian analysis argues that a properly attuned government can have a positive short- and long-run role, in preventing human errors from cumulating and cascading into either a 'Great Depression' or even a significant recession.

Keynes and Post Keynesians see government as not always and necessarily a corrupting force. It can be a corrective force, leaning against the winds of economic slump and coordinating human action to prevent depression and/or inflation. Post Keynesians also readily admit that if individuals were self-interested, but infallible, Turing machines in a world where the economic future was calculable, then they would neither make errors nor create new economic environments. Of course, then much of the joys (and sorrows) of life would disappear as we took on the characteristics of neoclassical 'robot decision-makers'. But as long as humans are human, and the economic future is uncertain, the responsibility of government, in the Post Keynesian view, is to encourage the human activities of creativity and productivity, while protecting society as a whole against actions which cause economic malfunctions. The government's role is discussed in more detail in the next chapter.

CONCLUSION

In sum this chapter presented some of the conflicting views between neoclassical and Post Keynesian economists regarding the entrepreneurial decision-making process and its implication for the role of government. If the logical assumptions of the neoclassical view are adopted as the starting-point of any economic theory, then observed real-world maladies where, for example, unemployment and inflation concurrently exist can only be 'explained' as a temporary aberration due to frictions, short-run price and wage rigidities, short-run asymmetric information among transactors, or random shocks to the economic system. In the long run, if government does not interfere in free market adjustments to economic afflictions, then the economy will right itself and achieve a state of full employment without inflation. (This conclusion is merely a result of the unrealistic assumption of the neutrality of money and the resulting Say's Law.)

The ultimate goal of all neoclassical modelling is to present an 'idealized state', with its permanent long-run equilibrium solution, while all neoclassical theorists start with the assumption that full employment and stable prices is the necessary long-run position of a market economic system.

Professors Arrow and Hahn, however, have mathematically demonstrated that in 'a world with a past as well as a future and in which contracts are made in terms of money, no [general] equilibrium may exist'.[18]

Implied in this analysis is the view that, if the Post Keynesians are correct in arguing that money and contracts are essential aspects of real-world economies, then one cannot logically demonstrate that free markets must end up, even in the long run, at a full employment equilibrium. Instead, those economies which are organized on a money contracting basis may settle down to equilibrium at any level of employment; that is, they may exhibit unemployment.

NOTES

1. G. Davidson and P. Davidson, *Economics For A Civilized Society*, W. W. Norton, New York, 1988, p. 104.
2. This is logically impossible in a world where the future is calculable and each individual is motivated by her own self-interest in a *laissez-faire* environment.
3. Delivery is, somewhat anticlimactically, permitted to occur in the future, but the possibility that the delivering party may be unable to perform is never thought of.
4. R. Radner, *American Economic Review Papers and Proceedings*, **60**, May 1970, p. 451.
5. Ibid., p. 456.
6. F. H. Hahn, *On The Nature of Equilibrium*, Cambridge University Press, Cambridge, 1973, p. 14.
7. Ibid., pp. 14–15.
8. J. Tobin, 'Theoretical Issues in Macroeconomics' in G. R. Feiwel (ed.), *Issues in Contemporary Macroeconomics and Distribution*, State University of New York Press, Albany, 1985, p. 107.
9. M. Friedman, *Essays in Positive Economics*, University of Chicago Press, Chicago, 1953, reprinted 1966, p. 15.
10. J. Tobin, op. cit., pp. 107–8.
11. R. E. Lucas, 'Tobin and Monetarism', *Journal of Economic Literature*, 1981, p. 563.
12. K. Arrow and F. H. Hahn, *General Competitive Analysis*, Holden-Day, San Francisco, 1971, pp. 356–7.
13. These additional bank deposits represent additional contractual commitments by bankers to honour sight drafts or checks.
14. J. M. Keynes, *Treatise on Money. II*, London, Macmillan, p. 220.
15. For a fuller explanation, see Davidson, *Money and the Real World* (rev. edn), Macmillan, London, 1978, pp. 221–8.
16. Different variants of neoclassical theory have invoked various *deus ex machina*, for example, a Walrasian auctioneer who guarantees that each individual can pay for all he or she contracts out of the earnings he/she receives, to avoid having people in their model face the problem of liquidity.
17. J. M. Keynes, *The General Theory of Employment, Interest and Money*, Harcourt Brace, New York, 1936, pp. 150, 161.
18. K. Arrow and F. H. Hahn, op. cit., p. 361.

7. The Neoclassical vs Post Keynesian View of Government

If one accepts the neoclassical presumption that immutable laws such as the neutrality of money and timeless probability structures exist – even if currently they are only incompletely perceived by human beings – then logic dictates that we should agree with politicians such as Margaret Thatcher and Ronald Reagan and leave *all* economic decisions to the individual survivors in the marketplace who can never make persistent errors about the underlying structure. Accepting the neoclassical presumption that information about the future always exists (and is learnable – at least in the long run), means that political liberals find it impossible to respond to Ronald Reagan's favourite rhetorical query, 'Why should the government know more than you as to how to spend your income?'

Yet during the Second World War, Keynes spent much of his time developing a foundation for a postwar international monetary system which would have rejected Mrs Thatcher's Panglossian view of free markets and her distaste for linking the sterling exchange rate with those of her major trading partners. And, clearly, Keynes would have rejected the Reagan rhetoric that a constitutional amendment for a balanced budget is necessary for free markets to assure full employment. Obviously, then, Keynes's policy prescriptions for a money-using economy must be based on a different logical foundation than that of neoclassical economics!

It is true that if the economic future is never completely predictable, then there is no basis for believing that government will always make better judgements (less errors) regarding future economic events and needs than individuals in the private sector. Government can, however, take a longer view of the needs of the community, whereas individuals in the private sector are more likely to be motivated by opportunity for a quick profit. Consequently, there can be a role for 'the public authority...[to] play a decisive part in determining the scale of investment operations'[1] in long-term projects in which the community agrees that there are prospective social advantages, even if there does not appear to be sufficiently quick profits to encourage investment by the private sector. This does not mean that government should become heavily involved in the micro-decisions of product design and output levels of specific commodities – that is, in state planning at the factory level. Nor does this imply that the state must own the means of production.

In the 'Concluding Notes' to his *General Theory,* Keynes wrote:

> I conceive, therefore, that a somewhat comprehensive socialization of investment will prove the only means of securing an approximation to full employment; though this need not exclude all manners of compromises and of devices by which public authority will cooperate with private initiative. But beyond this no obvious case is made out for a system of state socialism. It is not the instruments of production which is important for the state to assume. If the state is able to determine the aggregate amount of resources to augment the instruments *and the basic reward to those who own them*, it will have accomplished all that is necessary.[2]

In fact, in a system of state socialism, there are indeed great dangers in the loss of freedom and in a resulting lack of diversity and technological progress. There are some great advantages to a decentralized market system which we should not ignore. For example, it permits a creative private entrepreneurship, especially in a world where the government provides a safety net against the most dire of possible economic consequences when humans err. In the proper economic environment, as Keynes suggested:

> The advantage to efficiency of the decentralization of decisions and of individual responsibility is even greater, perhaps, than the nineteenth century supposed.... But, above all, individualism, if it can be purged of its defects and its abuses, is the best safeguard of personal liberty in the sense that, compared with any other system, it greatly widens the field for the exercise of personal choice. It is also the best

safeguard of the variety of life, which emerges precisely from this extended field of personal choice, and the loss of which is the greatest of all the losses of the homogenous or totalitarian state. For this variety preserves the traditions which embody the most secure and successful choice of former generations; it colours the present with the diversification of its fancy; and, being the handmaid of experiment as well as of tradition and of fancy, it is the most powerful instrument to better the future.[3]

Although a *laissez-faire* system tends to suffer from recurrent, and often prolonged, bouts of unemployment and/or inflation, and it tends to generate an arbitrary and inequitable distribution of income and wealth, nevertheless it has the potential to encourage product diversity, quality, technological improvements, and so on. Government's role is to create an environment which greatly reduces the defects of the economic system without eliminating its many advantages. Government can foster conditions which reduce uncertainties in financial matters, and it can act as an offset to limit, if not completely prevent, the dreadful consequences of antisocial economic behaviour.

When the private sector becomes too desirous of liquidity to promote full employment, the government can create the liquid assets necessary to quench desires while still encouraging full employment. When entrepreneurs lose their 'animal spirits', the government can create the financial incentives for management to invest in socially beneficial projects. When individuals' self-interests, buttressed by some form of market power, destabilize the existing distribution of income and thereby cause inflation and/or prevent an equitable distribution of economic gains among the members of society, the government can specify limits to self-aggrandizement. Finally, when individuals in pursuit of their own self-interest undertake economic activities which the community determines – by democratic processes – are uncivilized and not in the social interest, then the government must produce an environment which encourages voluntary as well as legal compliance with the civilized strictures of society.[4]

In modern democracies, government is, by its very nature, endowed with the wherewithal to pursue such a role. It can act in these situations because it is unfettered by the many accounting constraints placed on private enterprise.[5] As the enforcer of the civil laws and the regulator of the banking system, government is both the provider and ensurer of liquidity. These attributes provide it with the tools to act to eliminate systematic liquidity crises, while permitting individuals to experience episodic liquidity problems whenever society believes economic punishment of individuals is necessary to teach 'correct' economic behaviour in managing their individual affairs. Governments, free of balance sheet shackles, can stimulate private-sector productive entrepreneurship when necessary, while assuring that all members share in the fruits of the resulting economic prosperity.

In our modern democratic society, governments can take these actions as long as the citizenry do not revoke its charter to govern. Thus, for effective government action, it is not enough for politicians to be 'right', they must also be 'clever'. In other words, identifying the proper principles to guide government actions is not sufficient, the design of policy must be cleverly packaged so that it conforms as much as possible with the existing culture, habits and institutional history of the community and hence enlists community support. Cleverly designed public policies are necessary to encourage the maximum voluntary compliance with governmental legislation, if the objectives are to be achieved.

To secure an economic environment where full employment without inflation is possible, Post Keynesians insist that government can, and must, be permanently aware of the necessity to take action to encourage a positive and active entrepreneurial psychology. Whenever managers become too pessimistic about future economic events, they will not make enough hiring and investment decisions to ensure the full employment of society's productive resources. In such circumstances, only government has the ability, through its taxation, expenditure and monetary policies, to stimulate additional effective demand which, when properly designed, can shake entrepreneurs out of their lethargy and encourage them to expand hiring and productive economic activity. As long as there are idle workers and unused capacity, the capitalist system is not delivering all the goods of which it is capable! It is wasting available resources which could, if employed, improve the well-being of every member of society.

It is the responsibility of a civilized government to act as a balancing wheel in maintaining industry's aggregate sales by using its fiscal powers – that is, its power to spend and to tax – to make sure that total market demand neither stagnates nor declines. All civilized governments must assume the obligation to assure that:

(a)   current aggregate demand is sufficient to encourage business firms to create productive employment for all those who wish to work; and

(b)   guarantee that future effective demand will be sufficient to reward entrepreneurs who develop new plant and equipment to improve worker productivity.

Of course, any increase in government spending and/or tax cuts will force the government to increase its borrowing, thereby enlarging the government's deficit and expanding the National Debt. If the government borrows to finance additional expenditures on its own account, then this increase in governmental purchase orders pumps up the total market demand facing businessmen. Alternatively, if government cuts taxes this leaves consumers and business firms with more after-tax income, and some portion of this additional after-tax income can be expected to be used to buy additional goods in the marketplace.

In either case, therefore, the augmented National Debt will be associated with an increase in the total demand for the products of business firms. If such government 'deficits' are undertaken on a proper scale in any given recessionary circumstances, this can generate sufficient profit opportunities to encourage businessmen to expand production and employ idle machinery and unemployed workers. In this manner, then, the government can, by direct policy action, avoid the wasteful underutilization of productive resources by private enterprises and, in so doing, improve the economic well-being of its citizens.

For Keynes and the Post Keynesians, the absolute size of the government deficit necessary to achieve full employment is of secondary importance. It must be tailored to the potential unemployment problem at hand. In this Post Keynesian view, it is of no value for a civilized community to have government maintain a balanced budget while its citizens are impoverished because of a lack of opportunities to earn income. It is of great value to a civilized society to have a government that goes as deeply into debt as necessary to provide the full employment and prosperity of *all* of its citizens.

For neoclassical theorists, on the other hand, if they are going to be consistent with their logical basis, increasing the National Debt does matter! In the long run, if not sooner, government deficit must always cause inflation by excessively increasing demand. Since, according to Say's Law, income-producing supply activities always create their own demand, any government deficit must ultimately involve generating additional demand in excess of the long-run full employment demand of the private sector guaranteed by Say's Law. For logical consistency, therefore, neoclassical theory must view all permanent government deficits as an absolute evil.

Neoclassical Keynesians, who professed that neoclassical principles underlie their macroeconomic analysis are therefore forced, if they are to be logically consistent, to view government deficits as an ultimate evil. Such neoclassical Keynesians and Nobel Prize winners as Professors Robert Solow, Paul Samuelson and Franco Modigliani of MIT, and Professor James Tobin of Yale, cannot logically accept the Post Keynesian argument that the growth in the government debt is of secondary importance whenever the economy is unable to achieve full employment of its resources. Unfortunately for them, their common sense often gets in the way of their logic – often to the detriment of their consistency. Consequently, Neoclassical Keynesians must explain any actual deviation from full employment as only short-run and temporary – even though the adjustment process back to full employment may take an indefinitely long time to work its way out.

Thus, while their common sense leads them to recognize that unemployment is a real economic problem, their logic brings neoclassical Keynesians to accept the idea that it is really a temporary situation, and that, in the long run, the market will bring about full employment. Indeed, such 'Keynesians' could be described as merely impatient neoclassicists unwilling to wait for natural processes to create a state of economic bliss. This leads them into the schizophrenic situation of endorsing government deficit spending policies in periods of unemployment as a means of reducing the time needed for the adjustment process to run its course whilst also believing that government deficits should not interfere with the market solution in the long run. To resolve this common sense versus logical dilemma, neoclassical Keynesian dogma permits governments to run deficits in the short-run recessionary phase of the business cycle so long as these deficits are offset by budget surpluses in the prosperity phases of the cycle. For Neoclassical Synthesis Keynesians, then, the policy goal is to run a balanced government budget over the entire business cycle, so that, in the long run, the National Debt does not increase.

A neoclassical Keynesian rationalization of the necessity of running a balanced-over-the-cycle budget can be expressed as follows. The government deficits necessary to stimulate the economy during any 'temporary' period of unemployment results in increases in the quantity of money. The government must borrow from the banking system in order to finance the deficit and hence the banking system – under the direction of the Central Bank (the Federal Reserve in the United States) – will 'create' the money in order to permit the government to spend more cash than it takes in from the public. But since neoclassical Keynesians accept the long-run neutrality of money axiom, this increase in the 'neutral' money supply can logically have no long-run effect on employment and output. Neoclassical Keynesians are, therefore, forced by the logical results of their neoclassical money neutrality assumption to admit that, if there is a permanent growth in the National Debt, there must be a corresponding long-run growth in the 'neutral' money supply. Since the latter cannot increase long-run real output, it can only raise prices and thereby cause inflation.

The only way of avoiding this long-run inflation conclusion is for neoclassical Keynesians to argue that the government should balance its budget over the business cycle. This means that if the government runs a *deficit* during the recessionary phase of a business cycle, then the government should run a *surplus* during the prosperity phase. Over the whole business cycle, according to the neoclassical Keynesian approach, the government surpluses and deficits should cancel each other out. This would result in no increase in government debt over the business cycle, and therefore no need to finance permanently expanding government debt through a *permanent* increase in the money supply.[6] It therefore follows that, in the Neoclassical Synthesis Keynesian world of neutral money, balanced government budgets (over the business cycle) is a necessary condition for eliminating inflation in this neoclassical Keynesian, neutral money economy.

For Keynes and the Post Keynesians, on the other hand, money is *never* neutral. They believe that increases in the quantity of money are not *per se* a direct cause of inflation. Instead they argue that, in order to permit businessmen to expend additional sums on investment and hence stimulate demand and employment opportunities, businessmen must increase their borrowing from banks. This additional bank borrowing expands the money supply, which is a necessary condition for financing an economy where the production of goods and services is expanding.

If the private sector fails to provide this stimulus by refusing to increase its debt and borrow additional sums from the banking system in order to stimulate more production and sales, then the Post Keynesians argue that the government must increase the supply of non-neutral money and effective demand to ensure full employment. Whenever there are idle resources, government borrowing can increase the money supply to be used for expanding demand and encouraging business to raise real output and hire more workers in order to respond to this expansion. If output expands as a result, money is not neutral; and the increased volume of real national output implies that prices need not rise merely because there is also more money in the system.

If the Keynes–Post Keynesian argument is correct and so obvious, why then, the reader may ask, has government not diligently and persistently pursued a permanent deficit spending policy to ensure full employment? Since the Second World War, whenever the US government has pursued a consistent, sufficiently large deficit spending policy, a prosperous economy approaching full employment was perpetuated – for example, 1949–53, 1955–58, 1961–69, 1982–90. But, as full employment was approached, inflationary tendencies often increased. Faced with the threat of rising inflation levels, politicians tended to retreat from Keynesian deficit policies. The conventional neoclassical wisdom of the neutrality of money has then suggested that the cause of the inflation was an excessive creation of additional money supplies associated with the money used to finance the government deficits and that slowing down the growth in money supply by eliminating, or at least reducing, the deficit would not cause unemployment (at least in the long run). Hence, whenever inflationary pressures built up, politicians abandoned Keynes's approach for a foolish and largely unsuccessful attempt permanently to eliminate inflation from the economic system.

There have been two major exceptions to this generalization in the USA: the 1961–69 years of the Kennedy–Johnson administration, and the Reagan–Bush years of 1982–90. In both these cases a persistent, significant and deliberate deficit spending policy was pursued, and in both cases the economy experienced growth and prosperity without significant inflation. Despite differences in their rhetoric (clever packaging?), the Democratic Kennedy–Johnson and the Republican Reagan–Bush governments sustained successful economic performances without significant threats of inflation – for periods of at least 8 years.

In order to comprehend why these administrations could stimulate employment without exacerbating inflationary pressures, it is necessary to develop a theory of inflation. The next two chapters will provide a basic understanding of the conflicting views on inflation, and permit the reader to evaluate which better fits the 1961–69 and 1982–90 experiences.

NOTES

1. J. M. Keynes, *The General Theory of Employment, Interest and Money*, Harcourt Brace, New York, 1936, pp. 163–4.
2. Ibid., p. 378 (italics added).
3. Ibid., p. 380.
4. See G. Davidson and P. Davidson, *Economics For A Civilized Society*, Macmillan, London, 1988.
5. Government normally does not maintain a balance sheet. It does not value its assets and hence does not have to worry about the value of its net worth.
6. Since Ronald Reagan doubled the National Debt from one trillion to two trillion dollars (and the money supply soared correspondingly) during the early 1980s, neoclassical Keynesian logic would have required that the US government run a surplus of approximately one trillion dollars (and a corresponding reduction in the money supply) during the prosperous last half of the 1980s. Is it surprising, therefore, that no one hears neoclassical Keynesians espousing the desirability of the balanced-over-the-cycle government budget nowadays?

8. Three Views on Inflation: Monetarist, Neoclassical Keynesian and Post Keynesian

In the 1978 inaugural issue of the *Journal of Post Keynesian Economics*, Harvard Professor John Kenneth Galbraith attempted to explain what are the distinguishing features of Post Keynesian analysis. He wrote:

> Post Keynesian economics is amendatory and not revolutionary. It holds that industrial society is in a process of continuous and organic change, that public policy must accommodate to such change, and that by such public action performance can, in fact, be improved. Its commitment is to reformist change, not revolution, but it does not consider this commitment any slight or passive thing.
>
> The relevant historical change to which there must now be accommodation is in the nature of the industrial market. The market, with its maturing of industrial society and associated political institutions, loses and loses radically its authority as a regulatory force. Partly this is inherent in industrial development – in the institutions that modern large-scale production, technology, and planning require. Partly it is an expression of the democratic ethos, and paradoxically, this is often much applauded by scholars of liberal view who are also, and inconsistently, defenders of the market.[1]

For Galbraith, an important issue is the question of self-determination and control of one's economic destiny. He has argued that individuals have learned that they cannot have control of their economic lives when they leave the determination of their pay to the tyranny of a free market. Yet, in all modern societies with any democratic tendencies, people not only demand economic security from their economic system but also demand to play a controlling role in determining their economic fate. Galbraith noted:

Specifically, in the modern democratic context, people seek to gain greater control over their own lives. This extends to all of life's dimensions. They do not neglect the most obvious of all goals, which is greater control over their income. It would, indeed, be inconceivable were they to struggle for greater self-determination in all other aspects of life and leave this most vital dimension untouched.... The professional commitment [of neoclassical economists] to the market has, however, largely excluded from their view this struggle to substitute greater self determination of income for, as people of the modern industrial society see it, the impersonal tyranny of the market.[2]

According to Professor Galbraith, in modern times the market has become an institution characterized by power struggles for higher incomes between unions, political coalitions, economic cartels and monopolistic industries. If economists look to the market for resolving these conflicts, they are forced, according to Galbraith, into three possible choices:

The first is to deny that anything has happened to the market. In this way the validity of the existing market models is preserved in principle (and in the textbooks) though not, unhappily, in practice. The past is preserved at the price of increasing irrelevance. However, those so committed must on occasion wonder how long their convenient world will survive the evidence. Reality has a way of intruding on even the most useful of illusions.[3]

This first approach is chosen by proponents of pure neoclassical theory undiluted by any Keynesian flavour, for example, economists such as Professors Lucas and Sargent, and Nobel Prize winner Professor Milton Friedman. The fundamental basis of their economic analysis is the presupposition that, in the absence of government interference, market participants operate as if they were fully informed and perfectly competitive. They possess no market power. Neoclassical Keynesians such as Paul Samuelson and Robert Solow logically accept the neoclassical assumptions as the basis for their long-run analysis, but simultaneously believe that, in the short-run, economic power in the marketplace can lead to uneven and unhealthy income inequalities as well as slowing the hypothesized market adjustments to economic disturbances. These latter economists, according to Galbraith, opt for the second choice:

> The second choice is to accept that the market has declined but to believe it can be retrieved. So, in accordance to personal predilection, these economists urge the unwinding of government regulation, the abandonment of farm support prices, and the lowering of the minimum wage. And, of course, stronger enforcement of the antitrust laws is also demanded. This is, perhaps, the most compulsive act of piety. The disintegration of unions is not urged, although, in all logic it should be part of the obeisance. Even banality must be tempered with discretion....Genuflection is involved here, not practical action.... Neither the nonrecognition of the obvious nor the advocacy of the futile is a serviceable expedient.[4]

For Galbraith, however, there is a third choice, a more realistic one:

> There remains the third choice, which I think is central to Post Keynesian economics. That is to accept the decline of the market. Then one addresses oneself to considering how the resulting economic performance can be made socially acceptable to as many people as possible. That is my view as to what Post Keynesian economics is about.[5]

The Post Keynesian approach is amendatory then in the sense that it buttresses those aspects of the market system that still perform adequately well, while attempting to develop governmental and quasi-public institutions to moderate market performance which otherwise proves inadequate to the tasks at hand. But the Post Keynesians believe that, in a modern democracy, it is not possible to resurrect a free and unfettered marketplace to achieve all society's economic goals.

INFLATION AND INCOME DISTRIBUTION

If an entrepreneurial, market-oriented, money-using economy possesses an accommodating banking system and a government responsible for creating the demand necessary to ensure full employment, it can face a dilemma if the approach to full employment is associated with a rising rate of inflation. If people experience increasing inflationary pressures as the rate of unemployment declines under government deficit spending policies, it is not surprising that they will accept the belief that to fight inflation it is necessary to increase the rate of unemployment in the short-run up to a level where inflation disappears. Such a scenario, however, tends to support Karl Marx's claim that 'an industrial reserve army of the unemployed' is a necessary adjunct of a stable capitalist system.

However, Keynes believed that no-one had a legitimate vested interest in low (stable) prices if this was bought at the expense of permanent high unemployment. If we are to preserve the capitalist system in a political democracy, the government has a responsibility to promote a level of effective demand sufficient to approach full employment. The immediate question then is can capitalism achieve a non-inflationary state without having to perpetuate an industrial army of unemployed workers? In order to answer this question, one must analyse the relationship between money (and the banking system), the financing of aggregate demand, the costs of production and inflation. Keynes felt that he had provided an analysis which demonstrated that:

> ...the long-run relationship between the national income and the quantity of money depended on liquidity preferences. And the long-run stability or instability of prices will depend on the strength of the upward trend of the [money] wage unit (and, or more precisely of the cost unit) compared with the rate of increase in efficiency of the productive system.[6]

The previous chapters have developed the money–gross national income liquidity relationship. What remains to be seen is how economists have tried to untangle the phenomenon of inflation in relationship to production flows, production costs and the money supply.

Keynes and the Post Keynesians recognize that any banking system which can provide additional finance for managers to expand output is also capable of providing finance for managers to meet rising money-wage and other raw material costs which increase the money costs of production. How then does an economy, assured of full employment and a banking system ready to finance rising production costs, prevent managers, material suppliers and workers from raising the prices which they charge for their services in their own self-interest?

The neoclassical answer to this question is that there is only one way consistent with maintaining liberty in a society where people are motivated solely by self-interest. In a 'free' society, workers and entrepreneurs should be free to demand any price for their services, even if such demands are inflationary. As long as there is an obdurate, pre-announced limit to the growth in the money supply, banks will not be able to provide sufficient finance for maintaining production of the same level of output in the face of these inflationary demands. If some workers and managers raise their prices, the restraint on bank money creation means that there will not be enough money in circulation to buy the things that can be produced at these inflated prices. The resultant weakening of demand – a planned recession – forces managers to lay off some workers. The resulting 'natural rate' of unemployed will threaten the jobs of employed workers, thereby, according to conservative doctrine, curbing future wage demands to non-inflationary levels.

Post Keynesians challenge this view that it is necessary to perpetuate an underclass of unemployed in order to keep demands of the remaining employed at non-inflationary levels. Persistent unemployed workers are neither 'natural' nor necessary. Planned recessions are neither worthy of consideration, nor necessary as explicit policy goals for any society claiming to be civilized. To understand the basis of this challenge, it is necessary, in the rest of this chapter, to examine the relationship between inflation, income and employment as conceived by Keynes and the Post Keynesians. This can then be compared with the views of neoclassical scholars. Then in Chapter 9, our earlier discussion of money contracts can be used as a basis for explaining the 'good' and 'clever' anti-inflationary policies developed by Post Keynesians.

INFLATION AND INCOME

Inflation occurs when the prices of things we buy are rising - that is it takes more currency to buy the same volume of goods. Among the various price indices which attempt to measure inflation, the Consumer Price Index (CPI), which measures changes in the average price of goods bought by urban consumers, is the most familiar to the general public. The GNP price index is a broader and more comprehensive price statistic measuring changes in the prices of all the products that make up the nation's Gross National Product (GNP).

The GNP includes all domestically produced goods bought by:

(a)   consumers;
(b)   managers for investment purposes;
(c)   government; and
(d)   foreigners (exports).

Since the National Accounting System, which is used to measure GNP, is based on a system of double-entry bookkeeping, the 'double-entry' offsetting the value of gross national production is the value of the total gross national *income* of the economy. Any price increase associated with GNP must be accounted for by an identical increase in the prices (that is, wages, rents, interest, profits) paid to income earners. *Every price increase is an increase in someone's income.*

The GNP can be thought of as a huge pie (see Figure 8.1) 'baked' or produced by the combined efforts of workers, property owners, and entrepreneurs. Each contributor to the production of this pie receives, in payment for his/her efforts, a sum of money income. This income gives the recipient a claim to a slice of the GNP pie. The size of the slice claimed depends on the price of the productive services the contributor has provided. Consequently, if the money which income people receive increases more rapidly than the size of the GNP pie (the 'real' output), then the GNP price level must rise (inflate) to keep the National Accounts in balance.

Figure 8.1   Income shares of US GNP (1986)

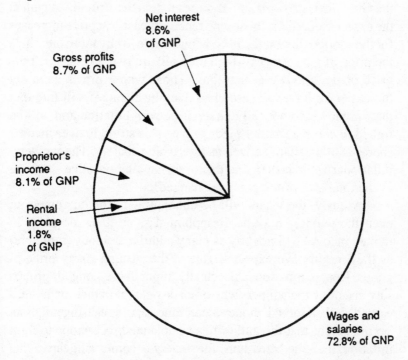

Anyone whose services are highly priced in a free market earns a claim to a large piece of the pie. Those whose services have a lesser value in the marketplace will earn smaller claims. The unemployed earn no claims at all. Individually, or as members of a group (such as, labour unions, cartels and so on), self-interested people can improve their relative living standards if they can negotiate a higher price for their services compared with the prices paid to others. If, however, the size of the GNP pie does not increase at the same time, then the gain in the slice of pie by any one group raising its price is at the expense of the rest of the community. If money incomes increase faster than the real pie grows, the accounting result is inflation as measured by the GNP price index.

Inflation is, therefore, a symptom of a struggle over the distribution of income. Whenever individuals or groups try to increase their share of the pie by contriving to raise their price faster than the GNP pie is growing, inflation results. In the struggle to gain at the expense of others, those who receive the largest price increases for the services they sell will be winners able to buy more pie, since the price of the services which they sell are rising faster than the price of the goods that they buy. Those whose prices have not increased (or have increased less than the average) will find that their money incomes fail to keep pace with inflation and will be forced to claim a smaller piece of pie. This struggle over income shares is often characterized as a zero-sum society. The winners' inflationary gain is offset by the losers' smaller pie slice – as long as the total size of the pie is unchanged.

Obviously, the losers will be unhappy with the outcome; but even the winners may be disappointed since their increases in money income will not buy as many additional goods (more pie) as they might have expected, due to the ensuing rising price of goods. Hence, inflation is politically unpopular among all groups – even among the winners who often do not regard their own 'hard earned' and 'deserved' money income increases as causing inflation. To the extent that the authorities use planned recessions to fight inflation, then the 'zero sum' for society becomes a negative one as the size of the pie is reduced.

According to the Post Keynesians, with the growth of an industrial society *and* democracy, people have learned that individuals and groups can and should attempt to exercise control over their own economic destinies. If one can gain some control of one's income, then one's destiny is largely in one's own hands. In the Post Keynesian analysis, there are three ways, in a modern society, in which individuals can affect and exercise some control over their income:

1. possess a unique, marketable qualification and exercise the monopoly power it provides;
2. organize with others who have similar market capacities in order to exercise some joint monopoly control; and
3. organize and employ political activities to tilt government policy towards improving one's income.

Professor Galbraith summarized these three forms of income control as:

> By organization, assertion of some unique personal capacity, or recourse to the state people win the power to set or influence their wage, salary, or other return, or the price which is one dimension of their income. By such means they escape from the impersonal authority of the market, or at a minimum, reduce the power of the market. Were it not that the market is a totem, the underpinning of all neoclassical orthodoxy, economists would long ago have reacted to this nearly universal effort, for they do not underestimate the desire for income and do not fail to appreciate its role as a liberating force. Their professional commitment to the market has, however, largely excluded from view this struggle to substitute greater self-determination of income for, as people of the modern industrial society see it, the impersonal tyranny of the market.[7]

In a world of big unions, big corporations, multinationals, international cartels and big lobbying groups, such as farmers, teachers, senior citizens and so on, each of these powerful entities can, and normally do, attempt to exert market or political pressure to increase its income at the expense of others. Post Keynesians argue that the existence of continuing inflation in any society involves some redistribution of real income from the weaker to the more powerful groups in an economy and/or its trading partners. For Post Keynesians, the occurrence of ongoing inflation is symptomatic of a struggle between organized groups, each trying to obtain a larger share of the available national or world income for themselves.

For example, in 1973 when the cartel of oil-producing and exporting nations, OPEC, agreed on a sudden reduction of oil exports to the oil-consuming nations, they were able to force up the price of oil from less than US$2 per barrel to US$15. Post Keynesians perceived not only that this was a highly inflationary trend in the world, but also that the resultant worldwide inflation was the instrument which permitted the oil producers to gain a larger share of the world's income at the expense of oil consumers.

The inflationary shock of the OPEC world oil price rise was then exacerbated by those oil users with market or political power, who demanded 'cost-of-living' adjustments to their income or fuel adjustment surcharges to the price of the products they sold so that they could afford the higher prices of petroleum products and still not diminish their purchases of all other goods. In other words, those who had economic power in the marketplace (or political power for those such as Social Security recipients whose incomes are determined in the political arena) refused to acquiesce peacefully in the redistribution of income that the OPEC price increase entailed. To the extent that households and firms received these cost-of-living or fuel surcharge adjustments, these powerful groups in society could maintain their standard of living and not lose income to oil producers. Of course, if some oil users increased the price of the things they sold in order to offset the oil price impact on their budgets, then the prices of their products and services rose, causing their customers to lose additional real income.

The struggle over the distribution of the US national income remaining after OPEC took its larger bite between 1973 and 1980, led to what Post Keynesians call a continuing wage–price inflation as each group in society tried to shift the burden of higher energy prices on to others. This dismal economic episode in US history illustrates the rationale underlying a Post Keynesian dictum, namely: 'Inflation is always and everywhere a symptom of the struggle over the distribution of income.'

THE POSTWAR INFLATION AND UNEMPLOYMENT RECORD

In the absence of an explicit political consensus on an acceptable distribution of national or global income, a fully employed *laissez-faire* economy cannot automatically harmonize the conflicting income demands of people motivated solely by self-interest. As long as there is always full employment, individuals need not perceive their inflationary wage and price demands as threatening loss of sales, unemployment and bankruptcies. Yet neoclassical economists have recognized that, in a free market environment devoid of any policy which directly limits income demands of various groups in the community, constraining inflation will require income losses, unemployment, the destruction of profits and a resulting reduction in the total size of the GNP pie – at least in the short run – in order to keep peoples' money income demands in their place!

The historical record shows that during the period 1961–68, and again briefly in 1972–73, when the government developed a consensus support of policies directly limiting money wage rate growth to the rate of real growth in the GNP pie (in other words, 'incomes policies') the US economy could and did approach full employment without suffering inflation.

During the Kennedy–Johnson years of 1961–68, prices were held in check by a wage–price 'guideline' policy which urged limits to money-wage increases. There were no legal punishments or monetary rewards to induce labour to limit its wage demands and behave in a socially responsible manner. The guidelines relied solely on the public voluntary compliance enhanced by President Kennedy's stirring inaugural request: 'Ask not what the country can do for you, ask what you can do for the country'.

For years, the guidelines worked! From 1961–69 the unemployment rate declined from 6.7 per cent to 3.5 per cent, while the consumer price level rose only 22.5 per cent (less than 3 per cent per annum) and the real GNP pie grew by almost 44 per cent (or over 5 per cent per annum) in those eight years as the result of increased government deficit spending resulting from a military build-up and a tax cut. With the escalation of the unpopular Vietnam war under President Johnson, however, the civic cohesion generated by the Kennedy charisma was shattered. Compliance with the guidelines disappeared in the last year of the Johnson administration as civic values were degraded and self-interest came to dominate.

For the next 13 years, part of the public agenda was a continuing search for an acceptable incomes policy to replace the 'guidelines' to control inflation and provide for an equitable sharing of the economic largesse of a fully employed society. Except for the seventeen-month period of President Nixon's wage and price controls beginning in August 1971, however, the main tool actually used to fight inflation was planned recessions induced by restrictive monetary policy. Between 1969–82 each tight money episode increased unemployment rates to what were thought to be politically unacceptable levels. With Congressional elections every two years and Presidential elections every four years, most politicians lost the political 'stomach' for the resulting unemployment and deserted the neoclassical cause of buying less inflation via higher unemployment. Consequently, as soon as the inflation problem began to abate, political pressures built up to restimulate the economy. As a result, the 1970s was a period of on–off restrictive monetary policies stringent enough to raise unemployment, but neither strong enough nor long enough permanently to subdue the inflationary struggle over the distribution of income. Until 1979 neoclassical tight monetary policy appeared to provide only a temporary respite from inflation.

In August 1971, President Nixon had successfully instituted a direct money incomes limitation policy via wage and price controls – a pragmatic approach which was, of course, in direct conflict with the expressed neoclassical philosophy of his administration. Since this incomes policy freed the Federal Reserve of responsibility for controlling inflation, it immediately eased monetary policy. The result was a vigorously non-inflationary economic expansion where real GNP grew at a rate in excess of 5 per cent during 1972 and 1973, with an attendant drop in inflation from 4.5 to 3.3 per cent. This vigorous recovery with less inflation contributed to the Nixon landslide election victory. When Nixon removed most of the controls after his re-election, prices climbed by 6.2 per cent in 1973 and by 11 per cent in 1974, making inflation again the principal economic problem on the public agenda

By 1975, President Ford felt the necessity to hold a 'White House Conference on Inflation' where approximately 700 leading US economists engaged in a two-day discussion of the problem. The only tangible result from this meeting was President Ford's WIN (Whip Inflation Now) advertising campaign which tried to emulate Kennedy's example of appealing to civic values. However, civic values had been eroded under Johnson's Vietnam War and Nixon's Watergate, and the resulting cynical environment prevented 'catchy' advertising slogans from whipping up public support.[8] Thus, the public saw the WIN campaign as a stunt, not a policy.

Unemployment increased from 4.9 to 8.2 per cent between 1972 and the planned recession of 1974–75. Inflation dropped to 5.8 per cent by 1976. With a recovery in the rate of growth in GNP and a drop in the unemployment rate from 7.7 per cent to 5.8 per cent in the early years of the Carter administration, however, the consumer price index rose to 6.5 per cent in 1977, 7.7 per cent in 1978, and 11.2 per cent in 1979. Inflation was again getting out of hand. President Carter therefore proposed a direct incomes policy – a 'real wage insurance' scheme – which would use the external incentive of reducing taxes for those who limited wage increases to a socially acceptable level. The Carter proposal, however, was abandoned by the President even before Congress could act.

Thus after Nixon's successful 1971–73 incomes policy, any suggestions for adopting an incomes policy were hesitatingly proposed and quickly abandoned. Restrictive monetary policy became the 'only game in town' to fight inflation. When inflation reached double-digit rates in 1979, the Federal Reserve – under a new chairman, Paul Volker – invoked a brutally restrictive monetary policy. Interest rates were pushed to unprecedented high levels, finance dried up, and loan defaults proliferated.

The result was to create a severe worldwide recession – the worst since the Great Depression of the 1930s. Unemployment soared from 5.8 per cent in 1979 to a peak of 10.8 per cent in mid-1982. The rate of inflation dropped from 13.5 per cent in 1980 to approximately 4 per cent in the last few months of 1982. In August 1982, when the Mexican government defaulted on its debt service payments to American banks, the Federal Reserve relented on its monetarist policy in order to prevent a collapse of the US and the developed world's banking systems.

The Federal Reserve was required to flood the economy with liquidity at the exact moment that Ronald Reagan's massive tax cut and expenditure growth policy took hold. The American economy and its major trading partners revived. By 1986, despite a much looser monetary policy, inflation had fallen to less than

4 per cent per annum; but the unemployment rate hovered around 7 per cent[9] until 1986, still higher than it had been for decades before Monetarism had been officially adopted as Federal Reserve policy by Mr Volker.

Inflation continued to decline, reaching a low of 1.1 per cent in 1986 but only at a great cost in terms of persistent high unemployment and significant unused industrial capacity. However, inflation had not been eliminated as an affliction of modern economies striving for full employment. In fact, by 1987 the first rumblings of a renewed inflationary era could be heard as unemployment declined to 6.1 per cent but inflation rose to 4.4 per cent. In the remainder of the 1980s, inflation edged up towards 4.6 per cent by 1989, while unemployment bottomed out at 5.2 per cent in 1988 and then slowly started to rise as the Federal Reserve attempted to slow inflation by cautiously increasing the tightness of its monetary policy.

AN ASSESSMENT OF THE MONETARIST EXPERIMENT OF 1979–82 AND THE REAGAN REGIME OF 1981–89

By August 1982, three years of very severe and lengthy monetarist policy had brought the international and domestic financial systems to near-collapse. With the fire of financial panic breathing down his neck, Federal Reserve Chairman Volker was forced to abandon this stringent monetary policy.

By 1986, with inflation running at 1.1 per cent, financial reporters regularly announced that the war on inflation had been won. This triumphant anti-inflation war successfully silenced any discussion of a direct incomes policy as an alternative to planned recessions. The economy did not require direct controls on income so long as society apparently accepted barbaric indirect controls of the price level via permanent high levels of unemployment.

The Reagan–Volker success doused liberal yearnings for full employment. Conservative dogma of the need for a permanent underclass of unemployed had become a socially acceptable doctrine even among liberal economists eager to share in the conservative success in fighting inflation.

For example, even though there were almost 8 million unemployed workers in the United States, on 1 March 1987 'liberal' Neoclassical Synthesis Keynesian economist and Nobel Prize winner Franco Modigliani wrote in the *New York Times* that 'we are now relatively close to the minimum level of unemployment that can be reached and maintained without a serious risk of rekindling inflation'. Modigliani unabashedly claimed that there was broad agreement among (employed) economists that not more than 1 million jobs could be filled by the 8 million unemployed without inflationary repercussions. In so doing, Professor Modigliani was expressing an accepted doctrine of Neoclassical Synthesis Keynesians. This Neoclassical Keynesian dogma based on an empirical law developed in the 1960s under the technical term of 'the Phillips Curve' maintained that there was an inevitable and immutable trade-off between unemployment and inflation. The Phillips Curve 'scientifically' demonstrated, Neoclassical Synthesis Keynesians claimed, that the closer any economy moved towards full employment the greater the rate of inflation it would experience. In Professor Modigliani's eyes, anything less than 7 million unemployed would put the United States on the dangerously inflationary segment of the Phillips Curve.

Apparently, Neoclassical Synthesis Keynesians, although closely identified with Democratic presidential candidates and liberal politics, were willing to sacrifice the economic lives of the remaining 7 million jobless to the immutable Phillips Curve law of economics that they had discovered! In reality, however, the economy continued to expand as exports rose in 1987 and 1988, and the number of unemployed fell to a low of 6.1 million in early 1989 without inflation significantly rising above the spring 1987 level when Professor Modigliani's article appeared. This aspect of neoclassical Keynesian theory was not borne out by fact.

While it is true that the inflationary battlefield was quieter in the mid-1980s than it had been in over a decade, the results of the war against inflation waged by the Reagan administration and the

Federal Reserve left the questions of how it was 'won', at what cost, who had won, and what were the spoils of that victory.

Much of the real credit for the mid-1982–86 recovery is due to the Reagan administration's policy of reducing taxes while *increasing* expenditures just as the Federal Reserve was reversing its stringent monetary policy in August 1982.[10]

Credit for the 1982–85 recovery should not be due to Chairman Paul Volker of the Federal Reserve and his relaxation of the high interest rates which he foisted on the United States and the rest of the world between 1979 and 1982. This 1979–82 Volker tight money policy forced the United States into the second largest economic depression in the twentieth century. Between 1979 and 1985 alone, the loss of real income to Americans from not running a full employment economy has been estimated at almost 3 trillion dollars.

In terms of our GNP pie analysis this means that had the United States managed to maintain a full employment economy, the average American would have had a 12 per cent larger slice of the pie *in each and every year since 1979*. This diminution in the relative economic well-being of the American people, due to the Federal Reserve's acceptance of the barbaric belief in the need to maintain a natural rate of unemployment, is truly staggering. Of course, had the Reserve not relaxed its monetarist policies in mid-1982, the resulting economic losses would have been more staggering.

The fuel that has been driving the Reagan–Bush recovery since mid-1982, according to Post Keynesians, has been the enormous federal deficits. Rather than constituting a new age of economic policy based on 'sound' finance, the recovery of the US economy between 1982 and 1990 is primarily attributable to a 'clever' repackaging of old Keynesian policy prescriptions of stimulating demand via deficit spending, plus providing the economy with sufficient liquidity via a less restrictive monetary policy.

Was Inflation Really Conquered?

Whatever victory against inflation has been achieved in the 1980s should be put into perspective. Inflation has declined from the double figures of the last year of the Carter administration to 4.4 per cent when Reagan left office and 4.6 per cent in the first year of the Bush administration. This 4+ per cent inflation rate appears to be 'low' when compared to recent experience. Nevertheless, an inflation rate of 4.4 per cent in mid-1971 traumatized President Nixon into imposing wage and price controls. Meanwhile unemployment remains close to the level of the mid-1970s and economic growth since 1979 was approximately 2.6 per cent per annum over the entire decade of the 1980s – well below the postwar 3.2 per cent average. Even during the Reagan 'boom' years of 1982–86 growth was only 3.3 per cent – about equal to growth averaged over prosperous times *and* slumps since 1946.

The anti-inflationary policies adopted by the Reagan administration are different both in degree and in kind from those of his predecessors. First, early in his administration, President Reagan made union-breaking respectable when he demolished the Air Traffic Controllers' Union. Although Reagan's anti-union stance was legal, for the previous 50 years (since Calvin Coolidge broke the Boston police strike in the 1920s), government officials have been extremely hesitant to use legal measures to bring about the demise of a workers' union and the resultant loss of market power by unions throughout the economy. The vigorous anti-union action by President Reagan altered the public perception of the permissible relationship between government and the wielders of labour union power that had been in place since the Second World War, severely weakening the militancy of the entire union movement in the United States. At the same time, the rate of unemployment was higher than it had been since the Great Depression. These changes significantly lowered the pressure for inflationary wage demands by workers.

Second, Reagan, unlike most politicians in the 1970s, stayed the course with Federal Reserve Chairman Volker's strong monetarist policy. The result was that, in the first 20 months of the Reagan presidency, the United States experienced the worst recession since the 1930s. Any improvement in economic performance was bound to look good after that dreary experience!

THE MONETARIST VIEW – BLEEDING THE ECONOMY TO CURE THE PATIENT

Professor Milton Friedman, the world's foremost monetarist economist, is usually credited with coining the statement that 'Inflation is always and everywhere a monetary phenomenon'. Friedman asserts that there is a *fixed* long-run relationship between increases in the quantity of money and the rate of inflation. This monetarist argument is ultimately based on the old homily that inflation is merely 'too many dollars chasing too few goods'.

This 'too many dollars' cliché is usually illustrated by employing a two-island parable. Imagine a hypothetical island where the only available goods are 10 apples and the money supply consists of, say, 10 $1 bills. If all the dollars are used to purchase the apples, the price per apple will be $1. For comparison, assume that on a second island there are 20 $1 bills and only 10 apples. All other things being equal, the price will be $2 per apple. Ergo, inflation occurs whenever the money supply is excessive relative to the available goods. The inevitable conclusion of this paradigm is that had the second island limited its money supply to $10, no inflation of apple prices would have occurred.

In this parable no explanation is given as to why the money supply was greater on the second island. Nor is it admitted that, if the increase in the money supply is associated with entrepreneurs borrowing 'real bills' from banks to finance an increase in payrolls necessary to harvest, say, 30 additional apples so that the $20 chases 40 apples, then the price will be only $0.50 per apple. If a case of 'real bills' finance occurs, then an increase in the money supply is not associated with higher prices but with greater output.

A tight money policy operates by raising the costs to bankers of borrowing funds; hence, bankers charge higher interest on loans to entrepreneurs. These higher finance charges increase managers' operating costs thereby reducing profit opportunities. This will reduce entrepreneurs' willingness to borrow to finance additional payrolls which, in turn, means that managers cut back on hiring and/or wage payments. This desire of management to shed labour may be exacerbated if managers interpret the higher interest costs as a warning signal that a recession is on the way.

If the resulting recessionary market environment forces workers to limit or reduce contract demands (so-called 'givebacks') during future labour contract negotiations, then the rise in production costs inflation will begin to slow. In the interim there will be a painful 'stagflation' – a stagnating production of goods with rising prices as some inflationary costs work their way through the system. Thus, in the United States, the Great Recession of 1979–82 produced stagflation during its early stages, while leaving a legacy of reduced wage demands in the 1983–86 period when inflation fell to 1.1 per cent.

If, on the other hand, the Federal Reserve does not develop a restrictive monetary policy when labour is demanding inflationary wage increases, then bankers can expand their loan operations. Accordingly, if a community vigorously pursues a full employment goal, while simultaneously having no societal limitations on people's inflationary income demands, then the economy has a built-in inflationary bias. This has led to the argument that an anti-inflationary tight monetary policy is the only alternative as governments' pursuit of full employment has created continuous incomes inflation pressures.

By creating unemployment, income losses and weak markets for goods, conservatives expect to make most people too weak economically to fight over the distribution of income. In puritanical terms, monetarists often suggest that such monetary discipline 'is good for the system' – comparable to the curative blood-letting practices of fifteenth-century physicians. Neoclassical economists and conservative politicians often acknowledge that recessions may inflict pain and suffering but, they claim, a stiff dose of monetarist medicine is needed to purge the system of those who would otherwise try to extort inflationary money income demands on the rest of society. In the long run, in true Social Darwinistic philosophy, this monetarist prescription necessarily punishes the lazy and makes industry leaner and more efficient.

There is, however, no evidence that after a planned recession the economy will *automatically* snap back to its (assumed) unchanged full employment growth without inflation, rather than languishing in a stagnating state of torpid growth or stagnation. By mid-1986, for example, despite almost four years of 'prosperous recovery' from the planned monetarist recession of 1979–82, the US economy continued to find itself operating at only 80 per cent of capacity and with 7 per cent of the labour force still unemployed – an obvious waste of potential resources. And, even by the end of the 1980s, the United States did not approach the low unemployment rates that the country had experienced in the non-recessionary years between 1946–70.

The intentional infliction of economic pain – that is, the use of planned recessions and losses in real income to keep inflationary income demands down – results in the economic maiming or even death of many innocent companies and people. Neoclassical economists claim that this pain is the inevitable price for fighting inflation. But monetarist policies that fight inflation via recessions are but one option. Post Keynesians argue that a civilized society should seek more humane ways to limit the income distribution conflict among members of its economic community, and that this conservative policy of deliberately hurting people should never be a first-choice solution for a civilized society. They feel that austere and unpalatable policies are not necessarily virtuous, and that planned recessions are the last resort of a failed civilized policy!

In stark contrast to the Post Keynesian view that inflation is a symptom of an ongoing struggle over income distribution by the exertion of market power is that of pure neoclassical scholars such as Professor Milton Friedman. In his book *Dollars and Deficit*, Friedman wrote:

> I should like to spend more time examining analytically the causes of inflation because the emphasis I have just placed on the stock of money as the culprit is widely regarded as old fashioned...modern writers today attribute inflation to very different kinds of causes...a wage push on the part of employees; or a profit push on the part of

employers and entrepreneurs.... If any of these factors produces a rise in the stock of money, it will produce inflation. But if it does not produce a rise in the stock of money, it will not produce inflation.[11]

Because of this view, Professor Friedman was quoted, in an 1974 article in *Newsweek*, as saying that there was no need for government price controls for petroleum products to prevent aggravating inflationary tendencies as US oil producers and companies tried to protect themselves against the OPEC price rises, since 'before the price of crude oil reaches $10 per barrel, the OPEC cartel would collapse'.

The basis for Professor Friedman's bold assertion regarding an OPEC collapse as a result of the oil price rise of 1973 was the implicit assumption that if the supply of dollars was not increased, then as oil prices continued to rise, consumers would run out of dollars – and hence there would be no one left to buy oil. Without any customers left who could afford the cartel price, OPEC would inevitably collapse. No one would be hurt, ultimately, except members of the cartel.

Of course, since Professor Friedman's analysis of the situation is based on accepting the neutrality of money assumption, then it logically follows the same global real output would be produced no matter what level the price of oil reached while consumers were running out of dollars. Hence sellers of other goods would have to accept whatever dollars consumers had left for their wares after spending their dollars on OPEC oil at its 'temporary' inflated price. Thus, while the OPEC cartel was in the process of sowing the seeds of its own destruction, according to pure neoclassical theory, the world would not suffer significantly, for all other goods would be continued to be produced – and be sold at significantly lower prices. This, the average price of goods would scarcely rise and the resultant inflation would be negligible. According to Professor Friedman, inflation could persist only if the Federal Reserve system flooded the US economy with additional dollars to enable buyers to pay the inflated dollar price demands of the OPEC cartel. In the long run, according to neoclassical theory, no real income would be lost as the neutrality of money assured that the refusal of the Federal Reserve to expand the money supply to pay OPEC's price demands would not impact real output and employment. If the Federal Reserve had accepted Professor Friedman's theoretical analysis, it would be difficult, if not impossible, to explain why a rational, logically consistent Board of Governors of the Federal Reserve System, committed to fighting inflation and pursuing long-run full employment, was willing to permit the money supply to increase in the 1970s!

So long as neoclassical economists such as Professor Friedman ignore the importance of any ongoing struggle by powerful groups in our economy over the distribution of income, in the belief that, in the long run, no adverse impact will occur while the Federal Reserve stands firm, they will have a hard time analytically evaluating the effectiveness of the policies advocated by Post Keynesians to fight inflation.

These Post Keynesian policies are labelled 'incomes policies', being designed to restrain and prevent any persistent struggle among the competing income demands of various groups, rather than an attempt to constrain the supply of money to limit inflation. As long as neoclassical economists assume the neutrality of money, then the only logically consistent policy recommendation for fighting inflation must be to limit money supply growth and leave the competitive forces of the marketplace to fight for the limited quantity of the consumer currency to determine the distribution of income by weakening the ability of buyers to afford to buy the full employment output of industry at inflated prices. Thus, politicians such as Margaret Thatcher in the UK and Ronald Reagan in the United States advocated no government interference with free collective bargaining accompanied by tight control of the money supply, so that any group of workers demanding and obtaining inflationary wage increases would be priced, with their entire firm, out of the marketplace. Short-run unemployment was seen as a necessary cost of keeping labour in its place! In the long run, however, neoclassical theory proclaims that there will be no economic losses.

Neoclassical Keynesians, as their name implies, occupy a middle ground between the pure neoclassical and the Post Keynesian approach towards the prevention of inflation. The neoclassical Keynesians accept the idea that if the money supply is constrained, inflation can be halted without jeopardizing full employment in the long run. But, in the short run, as consumers ran out of currency, sales would decline, inducing managers to lay off workers and close down factories – thereby pricing some resources out of the marketplace. This would predispose towards a great recession while the slow market adjustment processes mentioned by Professor Solow took time to right the economic system and workers and managers 'learn' not to make inflationary demands on society. Moreover, some of the workers thrown out of work, and some of the industries experiencing losses in sales, might not be those who demanded inflationary wage and price increases.

While the neoclassical Keynesian theory sides with Professor Friedman and the neoclassical monetarists in their long-run analysis, Neoclassical Synthesis Keynesians come out on the side of the Post Keynesians in the short run. For example, Neoclassical Synthesis Keynesian James Tobin of Yale has stated:

> Many mainstream Keynesian economists have long agreed that Keynesian macroeconomics cannot be grounded on pure or perfect competition in product and labour markets. As increasing numbers of them have come to the conclusion that wage and price controls or other incomes policies are at least occasionally necessary to prevent inflation at full employment, the practical gap between them and post-Keynesians has narrowed.[12]

Thus, it would appear that 'occasionally', according to Professor Tobin, an incomes policy is desirable. Yet the neoclassical Keynesians provide no analytical basis to suggest on what occasions, and for how long, such incomes policies should be pursued.

Post Keynesians, on the other hand, argue that the historical evolution of the twentieth-century industrial economic system with its developed financial system possesses *permanent* powerful economic groups in its midst. Pure or perfect competition is incapable of ever being realized in developed economics based on the economies of mass production, distribution and marketing. Hence if economies are to come close to producing their full potential without significant inflation in the presence of such powerful units motivated to improving their own self-interest, a *permanent* incomes policy is required. Only then can these powerful groups peacefully co-exist with the rest of the members of a civilized society.

Post Keynesians often compare the need for a permanent incomes policy to the need for a nuclear arms control treaty to avoid a nuclear holocaust. As long as there exist societies with the potential to launch massive destructive weapons, then it is more beneficial to global society that these groups have a pre-existing and permanent agreement to limit – and not use for first strike – their nuclear weapons. Rather than rely on a nuclear war to teach the survivors that even the winners are ultimately losers since they must continue to inhabit a world where nuclear destruction, economic poverty and deadly radiation become the spoils of war, a policy of arms control is desirable.

In contrast, the anti-inflation policy advocated by neoclassical logical analysis is to permit groups to make any claims they wish in the marketplace as long as governments avoid continuous deficits and limit the growth of the money supply to the expected increase in real output caused by increasing productivity and a growing population of fully employed workers. Theoretically speaking, this limited growth of a neutral money supply should have no damaging long-run real effects on employment and output in any economy operating under Say's Law.

The historical record, however, does suggest that there can be some important damaging real effects of a restrictive policy that limits the growth in the quantity of money under the presumption of neutral money. As we have already suggested, inflation in the United States reached a level of 11.3 per cent in 1979, following the second oil price push by OPEC in 1978 and the resulting attempt of domestic groups in the United States to shift the burden, via cost-of-living adjustments, fuel adjustment charges and the like, to the buyers of American products. In 1979, when Federal Reserve Chairman Paul Volker introduced a brutally restrictive policy to limit the growth in the money supply, interest rates were pushed to unprecedented high levels, finance dried up and loan defaults proliferated.

This drastic monetary policy was followed by the worst recession since the Great Depression of the 1930s. Unemployment soared from 5.8 per cent at the beginning of this restrictive policy in 1979 to 10.8 per cent in mid-1982 when the Volker tight money policy was finally relaxed. By that time, the rate of inflation had already dropped from 13.5 per cent in 1980 to 4 per cent – as workers were laid off, employers went bankrupt at rates unheard of for half a century, and the economic power of labour and industry weakened.

Neither neoclassical Keynesians nor Post Keynesians have ever denied that restrictive monetary policy can squeeze out inflation from an economic system by creating enough misery via unemployment, entrepreneurial losses and the resulting lack of profitable investment opportunities. But, unlike the pure neoclassical logicians, these Keynesian groups recognize that society will bear great costs not only in terms of unemployment and reduced real income, but also by the resulting slowdown in the accumulation of productive capital. These costs are considered too high relative to the 'benefits' of a successful anti-inflationary tight money policy, especially if alternative policies are possible which reduce inflation without these significant real costs.

Neoclassical Synthesis Keynesians, on the other hand, are driven by their 'bastardized' logic to argue that unemployment, business losses and the lack of profitable investment opportunities are a costly, but temporary, problem. In the long run, the free-market economy will restore full employment. Government action is urged merely to reduce these 'temporary' costs of unemployment.

Post Keynesians would argue that, given the evolutionary development of society, the only way of permanently reducing the threat of inflation via a tight money policy is permanently to depress the economy – to keep a permanent 'industrial reserve army of the unemployed'. Otherwise, Post Keynesians argue, if in a later period the economy again moves towards prosperity and full employment, the result will be to re-create or reinvigorate the powerful economic groups in our midst. All the while society not only permits but encourages behaviour based solely on the principles of self-interest, any economy which approaches full employment will encourage the powerful self-interest groups to attempt to improve their income at the expense of others – and the struggle over redistribution will be re-ignited. Hence, if we again follow neoclassical prescriptions, only another dose of bitter monetary stringency medicine will reduce the inflationary fever. Thus according to Post Keynesians, a long-run successful neoclassical anti-inflation policy requires that the economy be kept in a permanently semi-depressed state where high unemployment, high interest rates and low rates of capital accumulation are necessary for reduced rates of inflation.

Post Keynesians did not support the very restrictive monetary policies invoked by US Federal Reserve Chairman Volker in the period 1979–82, even though they recognized and admitted that if enough unemployment and business losses were forced on to the economic system, the rate of inflation could be reduced. Such policies of fighting inflation by deliberating causing severe unemployment and significant business losses are considered barbaric and antithetical to the success of the capitalist system since they can achieve their objective only by impoverishing society. Since 1982, for the remainder of the decade, although monetary policy has been somewhat more accommodating, Post Keynesians believe it has still been overly restrictive resulting in higher unemployment and lower capital accumulation than necessary. Post Keynesians advocate an income policy which would have permitted more employment, more profits, more accumulation and more prosperity without inflation as a civilized alternative to restrictive neoclassical monetary policy to fight inflation.

In Chapter 9, the basis for developing 'clever' Post Keynesian anti-inflation policies will be discussed. In the general context of our current discussion, an incomes policy involves a social agreement amongst the civilized residents of a society not to make inflationary wage and price demands on the rest of society. Although some have labelled calls for incomes policies as Utopian or unrealistic, Post Keynesians have attempted to devise policies which they believe are politically feasible and workable, *if* the government educates the public that if everyone fails to work together in a social contract to prevent inflation, everyone will suffer separately from inflation and/or the impoverishing neoclassical policy of fighting inflation through perpetuated unemployment, reduced real income and the retardation of capital accumulation.

According to the Post Keynesians, society can fight inflation while maintaining close-to-full-employment prosperity via incomes policies, while educating the public as to how these procedures will resolve the otherwise incompatible claims of each group trying to improve its income at the expense of others. The public must also be educated to understand that an incomes policy – and only an incomes policy – can, and will be, inexorably linked to a set of expansionary fiscal policies to achieve continuous full employment.

Public acceptance of an incomes policy will, therefore, guarantee maximum production and the highest possible standard of living for the community. The authorities have the responsibility carefully and clearly to explain that the only alternative to a permanent incomes policy is either permanent high unemployment (to limit inflation) or high inflation (which creates turmoil and destroys the economic system). Incomes policies are tools which allow the society to unleash its full economic potential without having to fear either of these consequences.

This view stands in stark contrast with the ideology of neoclassical theory which argues that government interference with the free market determination of wages and prices will destroy the efficiency of a *laissez-faire* system. It is for this reason that neoclassical Keynesians view incomes policy as a necessary pragmatic, but temporary, expedient for, if permanently used, they fear that the claimed efficacy of the 'invisible hand' of the marketplace will, in the long run, be crippled.

NOTES

1.   J. K. Galbraith, 'On Post Keynesian Economics', *Journal of Post Keynesian Economics*. 1, Fall 1978, p. 8–9.

2.   Ibid., p. 9.
3.   Ibid., p. 11.
4.   Ibid., p. 11.
5.   Ibid., p. 11.
6.   J. M. Keynes, *The General Theory of Employment, Interest and Money*, Harcourt Brace, New York, 1936, p. 309.
7.   Ibid., p. 9.
8.   President Carter experienced a similar disappointment when he tried to enlist public support for energy conservation by declaring it the 'Moral Equivalent Of War' without any positive leadership actions. The cynical public labelled the Carter moral equivalent policy 'MEOW'.
9.   Inflation in Europe also subsided but unemployment remained at a postwar high.
10. This success was not in any way related to the supply-side promise that the 1981 tax cuts, which would stimulate so much more additional work and investment, would pay for themselves. The huge and continuing federal deficit since 1981 is vivid evidence of the failure of supply-side economics.
11. M. Friedman, *Dollars and Deficits,* University of Chicago Press, Chicago, 1968, pp. 27–8.
12. J. Tobin, 'Theoretical Issues in Macroeconomics' in G. R. Feiwel (ed.), *Issues in Contemporary Macroeconomics and Distribution*, State University of New York Press, Albany, 1985, p. 116.

9. Buffers and Tips: The Post Keynesian Tools for Fighting Inflation

Using the discussion of the earlier chapters on the role of money and contracts in an entrepreneurial economy, it is possible to explain how to design direct and 'clever' policies to fight inflation without having to throw people out of work and businesses into bankruptcy.

SPOT-PRICE INFLATION

Spot prices require immediate delivery. Since production takes time, only goods which already have been produced and are currently being stored as shelf inventory can literally be sold in spot markets. Any sudden increase in demand for immediate delivery (or decline in shelf-inventory supplies) will cause a *spot or commodity price inflation.* The result will be a windfall change in the income of those possessing the existing commodities. The homily of the two islands, each with a fixed inventory of 10 apples and (sudden) different demands (assumed to be related to differing money supplies), is a simple illustration of such a spot-price inflation.

Buffer Stocks as a Solution for Spot-Price Inflation

Since a spot or commodity price inflation occurs whenever there is a sudden and unforeseen change in demand or available supply *for immediate delivery,* this type of inflation can easily be avoided if there is some institution, unmotivated by self-interest, which will maintain a 'buffer stock' to prevent unforeseen changes from inducing wild spot-price movements. This buffer stock is nothing more than some commodity shelf inventory which can be moved into and out of the spot market in order to buffer the market from disruptions by offsetting the unforeseen changes in spot demand or supply.

For example, since the oil price shocks of the 1970s, the United States has developed a 'strategic petroleum reserve' stored in underground salt domes on the coast of the Gulf of Mexico. These oil reserves are designed to provide emergency market supplies to buffer the US oil market if it is suddenly cut off from foreign supply sources. In such a situation, the spot price of oil would not increase as much as it otherwise would; a spot oil price inflation could be avoided as long as the buffer stock remained available. Similarly, if the United States had increased its purchases for the strategic oil reserves during the first half of 1986 when spot oil prices dropped from US$20 to almost US$10 per barrel as the result of worldwide excessive inventories of crude, the resulting oil price deflation, and its devastating impact on the income of domestic oil producers in the oil patch of the south-western states, could have been mitigated.

Although it may seem illogical that the US did not use the opportunity to buy additional 'cheap' oil to fill its strategic reserves during 1986, there are ideological and political reasons why it did not. First, additional purchases of oil would have increased government expenditures and therefore increase the government's fiscal deficit. Since the Congress had passed the Gramm-Rudman legislation in 1985 with the expressed aim of reducing the federal deficit to zero by 1992, increasing the deficit in 1986 – even to take advantage of bargain prices for oil – would not have been politically or ideologically acceptable to those politicians who think budget deficits are *per se* undesirable. Secondly, if the United States had increased its crude oil purchases significantly, the market price of oil would not have declined as much, and hence the rate of inflation, which fell to 1.1 per cent in 1986, would have been higher. Much of the extraordinarily low inflation rate that the United States experienced in 1986 was due to the decline in crude oil and the resultant fall in prices of gasoline and other petroleum products. Since the Republican Administration probably hoped that the experience of 1986 would demonstrate to the electorate that if they voted Republicans into office, inflation would never reoccur, they were unlikely to initiate policy actions which would have increased inflation.

In the absence of a commodity buffer stock policy, every unexpected change in spot demand or available supply will produce an immediate change in spot prices. In times of great uncertainty about the future use and/or availability of important commodities – for example, oil, metals, and so on – spot-prices can fluctuate dramatically and rapidly – as they did during brief periods in the 1970s and 1980s.

Rising spot prices signal an inventory shortage and thereby encourage an output expansion. The resulting rebuilt inventories will end the spot-price inflation. Falling spot prices signal to producers that inventories are excessive, and managers will cut back future production in order to work off the existing inventories, thereby arresting the spot-price decline. Essentially, spot-price inflation (or deflation) – provided that it does not induce change in the future costs of production – should subside as a result. However, to the extent that the spot prices of commodities are rising, it may take too long for new supplies to come to market. Buyers may not be able to wait for a return to more normal supply (demand conditions) or they may be stampeded by fears of an uncertain future into thinking that the current spot-price inflation will permanently affect future costs of production, thereby encouraging producers to raise their supply contract prices.

The policy solution to a spot-price inflation that threatens to outlive the buyers' patience is as old as the Biblical story of Joseph and the Pharaoh's dream of seven fat cows followed by seven lean cows. Joseph – the economic forecaster of his day – interpreted the Pharaoh's dream as portending seven good harvests where production would be much above normal followed by seven lean harvests where annual production would not provide enough food to go around. Joseph's civilized policy proposal was for the government to store up a *buffer stock* of grain during the good years and release the grain to market, without profit, during the bad years. This would maintain a stable price over the 14 harvests and avoid inflation in the bad years, while protecting farmer's incomes in the good harvest years. The Bible records that this civilized buffer stock policy was a resounding economic success!

Obviously the idea of using buffer stocks to stabilize commodity prices is not new. It was used briefly by the United States during the First World War, and was later revived as part of the New Deal agricultural policy to maintain farm income. Between the end of the Second World War and the 1970s, an expressed US government policy was to maintain significant buffer stocks of agricultural products and other strategic raw materials to support prices which adequately rewarded producers for efficiently organizing the production process. This US policy helped to stabilize commodity prices worldwide even as world demand for foodstuffs and other basic commodities exploded under the stimulus of global economic growth.

The other side of the coin of stable commodity prices was stable incomes for farmers and other commodity producers. This brought:

(a)   prosperity for raw material producers;
(b)   encouragement of continuing productivity-enhancing investment in these areas; and
(c)   a non-inflationary price trend for the food and basic commodity component of the consumer's budget despite a soaring global population and rapid worldwide economic growth.

In fact, from hindsight it is clear that the stability of commodity prices was an essential aspect of the unprecedented prosperous economic growth of the world's economy over the quarter of a century following the Second World War.

The success of this post-Second World War buffer stock programme over several decades, however, was its ultimate undoing. As productivity in food and other primary products increased (encouraged by a guaranteed price), some taxpayers began to object to the cost of carrying the buffer stock. Objections were also raised to the idea that the incomes of farmers and other commodity producers was being guaranteed at what appeared to be the consumers' expense. After all, if the existing surplus buffer stock was dumped onto the market, spot prices would fall, providing the consumer with a 'bargain' – at the expense of producers.

Public attention was not drawn to the fact that the urban taxpayer, as a consumer, received the benefit of a plentiful food supply at stable non-inflationary prices. And as workers and entrepreneurs in the industrial sector, they had plenty of job opportunities producing the many industrial products that only prosperous raw material producers could demand.

When the Nixon administration dismantled these buffer stock programmes in order to save warehousing costs and to use these savings to help finance the war in Vietnam, world spot commodity markets were left to the mercy of unforeseen and unforeseeable events. The result was the violent commodity price fluctuations that occurred in the 1970s and 1980s. In the early 1970s – even before the first oil price shock – world spot food prices began to soar as a result of natural disasters that reduced harvests and fishing catches. Since world commodity supplies were no longer buffered, prices swung wildly in response to these unforeseen disasters. As the buffer stocks disappeared, cartels of producers had the freedom to raise prices by restricting supplies. Cost-of-living escalator clauses in many wage contracts were triggered by this commodity inflation thereby causing this spot-price inflation to spill over into production costs (incomes) inflation for industrial goods. This process was already well under way in 1972 even before the OPEC oil cartel's embargo drove oil prices through the roof, and exacerbated the situation.

As a result, many nations who were net importers of agricultural products and petroleum were especially hard-hit by the ongoing worldwide commodity inflation. In the absence of any significant international buffer stock, each nation attempted to become more self-sufficient in these basic commodities rather than pay 'exorbitant' prices to the traditional foreign producers. This policy of self-sufficiency meant subsidizing less efficient domestic raw material producers. This self-sufficiency movement was further fanned by the Carter grain embargo in 1979 which signalled foreign grain importers that, for political reasons, they could no longer count on United States production to feed their population at any price!

These politically motivated actions by the Nixon and Carter administrations eliminated the United States as the world's major buffer stock operator who had, for decades, maintained international spot commodity price stability. When the United States abandoned the role of the world's non-profit buffer stock operator, commodity producers and consumers were given a clear signal that their future prosperity could no longer be secured on the civilized post-Second World War international institutions. Between 1945 and 1972, the United States' acceptance of the role of buffer stock coordinator in many internationally traded raw materials had contributed dramatically to the development of an international social agreement which had guaranteed profitable prices for basic commodity producers and the promise of especially good profits for those who searched out the most efficient production methods. In return the consumer received plentiful supplies, without inflation. Under this social regime, the global production and consumption of basic commodities involved a positive-sum game with both producer and consumer groups sharing in the resulting economic gains. When this collapsed, producers' prosperity began to depend on their ability to form coalitions against consumers to extract income from them – at best, a zero-sum game.

As the postwar international economic cooperative system broke down, many of the efficiencies of a civilized world were lost. To counter soaring basic commodity prices, many nations subsidized inefficient domestic producers. The result was that the world's production for many basic food commodities expanded and excesses came on to world markets just when the United States and then most of the rest of the industrial world were plunged into the great recession of 1979–82. This led to a startling commodity spot-price deflation in the early 1980s. As a result, agricultural and energy prices in the United States and worldwide plunged, bringing the US agricultural and petroleum sector to the brink of disaster.

If we have learned anything from this history of commodity price gyrations, it is that wild commodity spot-price swings in free markets create havoc, inefficiencies and misery – sometimes among producers and sometimes among buyers. At any point in time these volatile spot-price movements produce some winners and offsetting losers between producer and consumer groups, giving the impression that it is the zero-sum game. But from a longer prospective, the whole world has been a loser as a result of the unbuffering of commodity prices under the Nixon presidency, when compared with the world's economic performance from 1945 to 1969 when spot-price stabilization was an explicit policy goal.

INCOMES INFLATION

Changes in wages and material costs in production contracts always involve someone's income. With slavery illegal in civilized societies, the money–wage contract for hiring labour is the most universal of all production prices. Labour costs account for the vast majority of production contract costs in the economy, even for such high-technology products as NASA spacecraft. That is why inflation associated with production prices are usually associated with wage inflation.

Wage contracts specify a certain money wage per unit of time. For example, a secretary may earn US$10 per hour. If, during the hour, the secretary types 20 letters, then the unit labour cost of each letter is US$0.50. This labour cost, plus a profit margin or mark-up to cover material costs, overheads and profit on the investment, becomes the basis for managerial decisions as to the price they must receive on a sales contract in order to make the undertaking worthwhile. If money wages rise relative to the productivity of labour, then the labour costs of producing output must increase. Consequently, firms must raise their sales contract price if they are to maintain profitability and viability. When production costs, and hence contract prices, are rising throughout the economy, we are suffering from *incomes inflation*.

A PROPOSAL FOR A TAX-BASED INCOMES POLICY (TIP)

To prevent an incomes inflation requires some method of limiting money–wage rate (and gross profit margin) increases.[1] In 1970, Professor Sidney Weintraub laid out a simple, but clever, anti-incomes inflation policy which he called TIP or a *Tax-based Incomes Policy*. TIP made use of both civic values and self-interest, although the latter were more prominently displayed in the proposal. TIP is designed to counter inflation by placing a tax penalty, as a disincentive, on those companies that grant wage increases in excess of a socially acceptable non-inflationary norm based on average labour productivity increases.

The basic philosophy of TIP is that wage increases in excess of productivity growth will harm all members of society, and hence violates a basic civic value. Firms that accede to inflationary wage demands are inflicting a cost on the entire society, similar to that of polluters when they discharge wastes into the air or public waterways. Weintraub's penalty TIP charges enterprises for the 'economic pollution' produced by granting inflationary wage increases.

Entrepreneurs who accept inflationary wage demands at the bargaining table would be punished for their indiscretion. But the punishment differs from that inflicted by monetarist policy. TIP involves disincentives (higher taxes) levied directly on those whose behaviour fosters inflation. To offset the extra tax revenues paid by those penalized under TIP, those firms and workers whose behaviour was not inflationary would receive incentive rewards in the form of a tax cut. Under monetarist anti-inflation policy, on the other hand, punishment is inflicted indiscriminately on the entire community; workers are thrown out of jobs whether their specific behaviour was inflationary or not. Tight monetary policy bites by reducing the entire community's income and idling significant resources so that the community cannot buy as much of the GNP pie as before.

Once instituted, TIP would have to be a permanent policy institution if the inflationary dragon is to be permanently tamed.

There must always remain on the books a civic statement of acceptable non-inflationary behaviour as a constant reminder that inflating one's income is always contrary to the governing social interest. If a specific future date for the end of TIP was to be announced, its effectiveness would diminish as that date approached. Everyone would be told, in effect, that soon constraints on inflationary income behaviour will disappear. The existing social contract would erode as each member of society could no longer rely on the civilized behaviour of others. Self-interest alone would encourage each person to try to increase their own money income *before* others did so first. The struggle over the distribution of income would be re-ignited – and could be dampened only by the dousing waters of a planned recession.

Credibility and Compliance with TIP

TIP is based primarily on the use of the disincentives of tax penalties for anti-social behaviour. But it also mixes education and other social incentives to reform behaviour in a manner similar to the way road regulations govern driving behaviour on a country's highways. Speed limits, for example, are permanent but the magnitude of the speed limit can change depending on driving conditions, the need for energy conservation, and the like – factors whose *raison d'être* in achieving society's goals are clear to an educated driving public. Similarly, TIP would be a permanent institution but the magnitude of the allowable wage increase could vary depending on economic conditions, just as the speed limit can vary with weather and road conditions. Public education would be necessary to explain the factors affecting the magnitudes involved in TIP.

Speed limits, paying one's taxes and similar civic behaviour, depend to a considerable extent on voluntary compliance working in tandem with fines levied on those who excessively violate the rules. Governments never reward good drivers for not exceeding the speed limit or taxpayers for paying their proper taxes, since that is expected social behaviour of all citizens – even if it is not in their own self-interest. Similarly, those whose wage and income increases are non-inflationary would not be rewarded— such social behaviour would be expected.

Civilized governance relies on a coordination of enforcement with social norms. Sanctions work best when their primary function is to guarantee that social norms will not be taken lightly. This provides social norms with the credibility to develop; and it prevents the erosion of the norms by 'scoff' laws.

The institution of TIP would violate the current norms of both unions and business firms who believe in 'free collective bargaining' – that is, wage negotiations without government interference – just as a pollution tax can violate the norms of environmentalists who believe that polluting is an absolute evil and therefore no one should be permitted to pollute the air or waters merely because the polluter can afford the charge. Consequently the implementation of TIP must be accompanied by a strong effort to earn credibility in the eyes of both entrepreneurs and labour. Accordingly, implementation policies would involve four broad areas.

1. Entrepreneurial fears of massive government regulation and additional record-keeping requirements must be assuaged. Weintraub's TIP proposal was to be applied to only the top 2,000 firms in the United States. These firms produce over half of the GNP and are key to the general wage level and profit margins set in the rest of the economy. Since managerial control of such large enterprises already requires extensive record-keeping, TIP would not add to this burden as compliance could be calculated from existing records and shown on an additional three or four lines on corporate income tax forms. Smaller businesses – and especially new enterprises – on which the vitality of the entrepreneurial system depends would not be directly affected by TIP at all.

2. The public must be educated to understand that TIP will be inexorably linked to a set of expansionary fiscal policies. Acceptance of TIP therefore guarantees maximum production and the highest standard of living possible for the community. It must be carefully explained that the only alternative to a permanent incomes policy is either permanent high unem-

ployment (to limit inflation) or high inflation (which creates turmoil and destroys the feeling of belonging to an economic community of interest). TIP is the tool which allows the society to unleash its full economic potential without having to fear either of these consequences.

3.   TIP must have credibility. It must possess a simple structure so that the public can comprehend what is being implemented. Business, labour and the general public must be assured that TIP represents a ubiquitous social norm in the sense that:

(a)   TIP will not be vulnerable to political manipulation; it will not create a new arena where individuals and groups compete for higher incomes through political pressure or backroom deals.

(b)   TIP will not be vulnerable to non-compliance resulting from accounting gimmicks and other misrepresentations which hide excessive wage and price increases of dishonest firms while penalizing workers and entrepreneurs of honest companies;

(c)   TIP will not grossly distort the economy by creating a new set of strange incentives.

4.   TIP must be recognized as a permanent part of the economic landscape.

Transitional Problems in Installing TIP

Those whose money income status is caught in the transition from the current situation of free collective bargaining for wages and free setting of prices to a TIP relation must be treated fairly. This suggests that it will be easier to institute TIP during a period when inflationary forces are not strong (as in the 1980s). Whenever the ongoing struggle regarding income redistribution is lowered (perhaps as a result of the great recession of 1979–82) , however, it may appear that there is less need for a TIP policy. But if we are to avoid permanent slow growth or stagnation then a direct incomes policy is essential. The United States, and most of the rest of the industrial world, had an especially attractive window of opportunity for instituting TIP during the 1980s (as compared with the 1970s when it was clearly needed, but when the transition would have been especially difficult).

It is always difficult to transmute human nature – especially as it has developed in our entrepreneurial economy in recent decades. Although it is necessary to develop a core of civic values around the need to stop inflationary income demands, it would be foolish to rely solely on civic values. TIP will have to rely primarily on fiscal incentives as well. This is not a fatal problem. Societies often develop institutions which draw significant support for their existence and acceptance from related – but separated – civic values. For example, there is no necessary gain in self-interest in donating money to charity. As Dicken's self-interested entrepreneur, Ebenezer Scrooge, recognized the more one gives to charity the less one has for oneself. Only within a larger framework of a social agreement which values charitable contributions highly can there be an incentive to override self-interests and behave philanthropically.

To promote the civic values which TIP requires to operate effectively, the linkage must be made between TIP and the larger civic virtue of providing an environment in which it is possible to attain a non-inflationary full employment economy.

IMPORTED INFLATION

Until this point, our discussion of inflation has implicitly assumed that price increases are always associated with the prices of domestically produced goods. Yet when nations trade with other nations, rising prices of goods brought from abroad can result in an *imported inflation*. Although a complete discussion of the ramification of international transactions would take us far beyond the confines of this book,[2] it is useful to summarize briefly how inflation can be imported.

Imported inflation occurs when the price of imported goods rises in terms of the domestic currency. If there is a fixed exchange rate (that is, where the amount of domestic currency paid for a unit of foreign currency does not change over time), then any inflation which occurs in the exports of a foreign country will raise the cost of imports in terms of domestic money. The rising cost of imports in this case is due to either a spot or incomes inflation in the products sold by the foreign nation.

One of the conservative arguments against a fixed exchange rate system has been that such a system would therefore transmit spot or commodity inflation across national boundaries. Consequently, monetarists and other neoclassical economists have recommended a flexible exchange rate system (where the amount of domestic currency paid for a unit of foreign currency varies), so that, it is claimed, any inflation in the other country will automatically cause a *pari passu* drop in the amount of domestic currency paid for a unit of foreign money, thereby insulating domestic markets from importing inflation.

This claim of insulation was used by conservatives as a justification for encouraging President Nixon to move from the fixed exchange rate system developed after the Second World War to a flexible exchange rate system in 1972. Recent history has shown, however, that a flexible exchange rate system *per se* has not insulated the domestic economy from importing inflation. Any time that there is a significant reduction in the exchange rate of the domestic currency vis-à-vis the foreign currency, there has been an imported inflation – even if there is no change in the foreign production costs and foreign prices charged by foreign suppliers. In other words, experience has shown that a flexible exchange rate system is merely a way to redistribute income among nations – and thereby cause inflation in the nation whose currency value is falling in value on the foreign exchange market.

CONCLUSION ON A CIVILIZED ANTI-INFLATION POLICY

To paraphrase that old sage, Benjamin Franklin, if as a community we don't all hang together to fight inflation, then we will all hang separately via barbarous monetarist anti-inflationary policy.

Civilized policies to handle inflation rely on us acting as a community – both within our nation and amongst the civilized nations in our global community. One of the most important functions of government in any anti-inflationary struggle is to educate the public that any ongoing income distribution struggle is ultimately costly for all. It is a mug's game – a no-win, everyone loses negative-sum game – although at any point in time there may appear to be some winners.

In the absence of a sensible incomes policy to provide a civilized resolution to the income distribution question, the result is not a zero-sum game, but a real loss in total income as governments pursue restrictive monetary and/or fiscal policies which feed back depressionary forces on each other.

NOTES

1. Between the end of the Second World War and the oil and other commodity price shocks in the 1970s, the major inflation problem experienced by the United States was primarily due to money wages increasing at a more rapid rate than productivity increases. From the early 1970s to the early 1980s, however, profit margins also rose substantially.
2. For a complete discussion of these international aspects, see P. Davidson, *International Money and The Real World* (rev. edn), Macmillan, London, forthcoming.

10. Which Economic Theory for the Twenty-first Century?

John Maynard Keynes believed that economists should attempt to model the actual state of the real world in which we live – rather than an idealized long-run unrealistic system. As we have seen, Keynes believed that the tendency of neoclassical scholars to develop long-run solutions for real-world economic problems was not very useful. In his most widely quoted passage he held that:

> But this long run is a misleading guide to current affairs. In the long run we are all dead. Economists set themselves too easy, too useless a task if in tempestuous seasons they can only tell us that when the storm is over the ocean is flat again.[1]

Members of the Post Keynesian school insist that economic theory must deal with problems in an institutional, historical time setting where uncertainty regarding future events colours current economic decisions and actions. The political, social and economic institutions of a non-neutral monetary system and the use of forward contracts represent fundamental aspects of the world which we inhabit and must play pivotal roles in any economic model that we develop.

The idealized economic system embedded in the neoclassical model of the economy, on the other hand, involves a fully anticipated, statistically predictable future. Hence money, time and the need for liquidity play no important roles in determining real output and employment. Post Keynesians argue that since the neoclassical world cannot exist, even as an ideal, in the temporal setting of the real world, its results should not be used by policymakers. Keynes indicated that neoclassical 'teaching is misleading and disastrous if we attempt to apply it to the facts of experience'.[2]

In this brief book the reader has been provided with the foundations underlying the views of three important schools of economists: Neoclassicists and Neoclassical Monetarists, Neoclassical Synthesis Keynesians, and Keynes and the Post Keynesians. It is up to the reader to judge whether the neoclassical or the Post Keynesian logical approach provides better clues to the solutions of the economic problems that we will be facing at the close of the twentieth century and the beginning of the twenty-first.

The reader should remember that:

...the ideas of economists and political philosophers, both when they are right and when they are wrong, are more powerful than commonly understood. Indeed the world is ruled by little else. Practical men, who believe themselves to be quite exempt from any intellectual influences, are usually the slaves of some defunct economist. Madmen in authority, who hear voices in the air, are distilling their frenzy from some academic scribbler of a few years back. I am sure that the power of vested interests is vastly exaggerated compared with the gradual encroachment of ideas....But, soon or late, it is ideas, not vested interests, which are dangerous for good or evil.[3]

NOTES

1. J. M. Keynes, *A Tract on Monetary Reform*, reprinted in *The Collected Writings of John Maynard Keynes*, vol. IV, Macmillan, London, 1972, p. 65.
2. J. M. Keynes, *The General Theory of Employment, Interest and Money*. Harcourt Brace, New York, 1936, p. 3.
3. Ibid., p. 383–4.

Index